THE WHISPER OF A MILLION LEAVES

BEATRICE HAVERICH

DAMIANI

revive™

Smurfit Kappa
Townsend Hook

Robert Horne Group

Revive Silk combines impressive environmental credentials with a superb print surface. 75% of the fibre used in the production of this grade comes from paper that has been printed on before. Thanks to a sophisticated de-inking process and tightly controlled production procedures Revive Silk performs and prints like a virgin fibre grade.

Revive Silk is exclusively produced in the UK by Smurfit Kappa Townsend Hook. This mill has a strong track record in the collection and use of waste materials. They currently handle over 800,000 tonnes of waste every year which they convert into packaging.

Revive Silk is exclusively stocked in the UK by the Robert Horne Group - for more information about the whole Revive family please visit: www.roberthorne.co.uk

Damiani Editore
Via Zanardi, 376
Tel. +39.051.6350805
Fax +39.051.6347188
40131 Bologna - Italy
www.damianieditore.it
info@damianieditore.it

Coordination
Giuseppe Villirillo

Bookdesign
Beatrice Haverich

ISBN 88-89431-43-1

Printed on revive silk 170 gr.

Challenge, Survival, Transform, Reclaim, Participate.

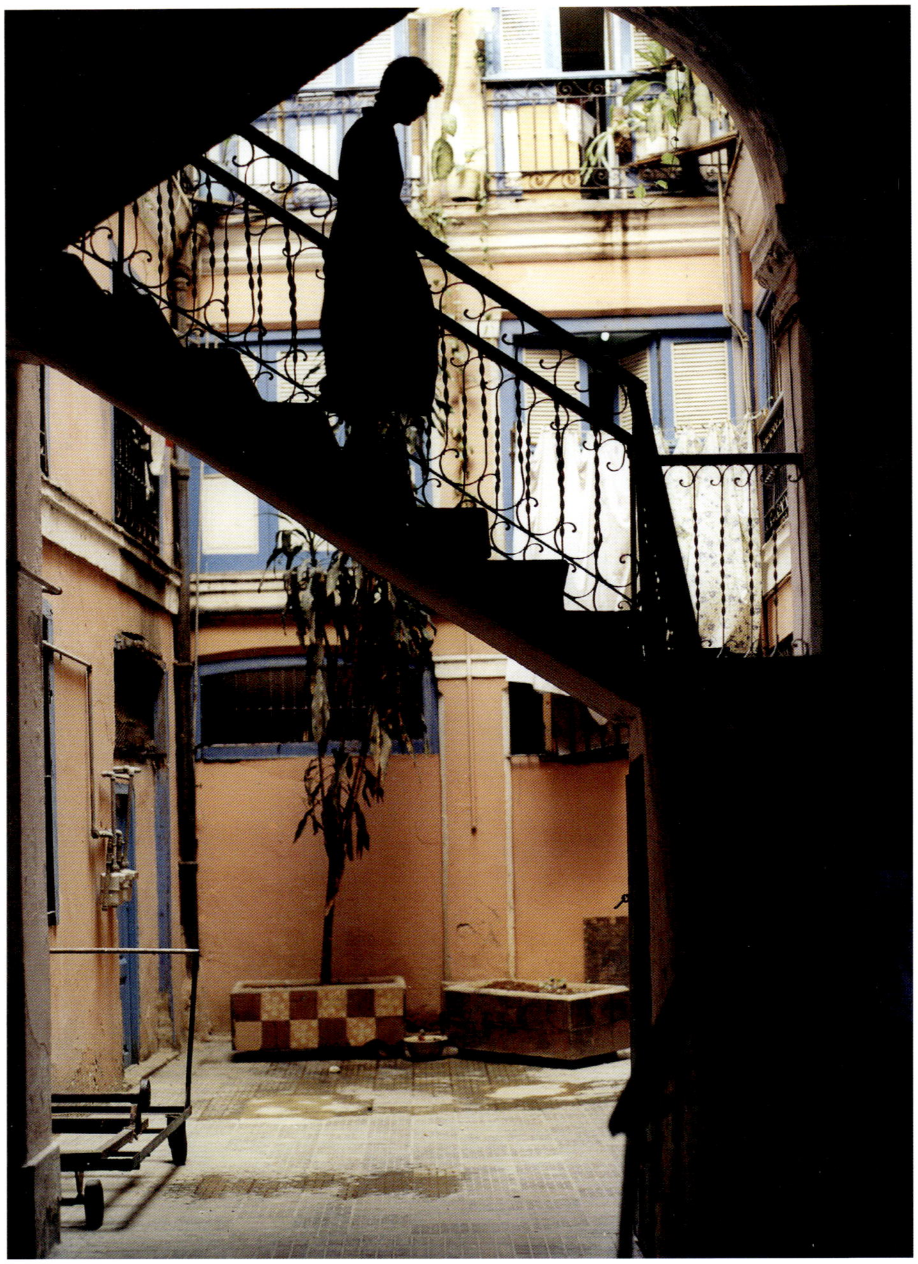

The sheer power of the dense backlit acacia leaves that confront you upon opening this book speaks eloquently to its central theme. It is in praise of trees, together, alone, cherished, ignored. Beatrice Haverich reveals and reveres them whatever their circumstance. But the book speaks to a wider cause too, that of the place of the tree in the wider environment generally, and in human lives specifically.

What shines through this book is the incredible tenacity of the tree. Clinging to rocky out crops; standing tall in the urban jungle; propped with long poles in elegant old age.

The human remains the greatest threat to the tree. Logging goes on at a furious rate from Indonesia to Brazil. Yet there are signs that things could change for the better. British Columbia's one of Canada's rugged Westerly states has just declared a swathe of land twice size of Belgium free from logging. The millionaire publisher, Felix Dennis is currently planting one of the largest forests in recent British history in and around the county of Warwickshire. But in the first decade of the 21st century, the world-wide inventory still shows infinitely more trees being felled than planted.

My own obsession, beyond the saving fo the rain forests - a big enough challenge on its own - is the propagating of the urban tree. In some ways the citizen in the developed world has more chance of saving or extending the presence of the urban tree.

Virtually every major city in the developed world is digging up its streets to put down new sewers, gas mains, and carbon fibre communications systems. London alone expects the utility companies to dig up some 30 km of streets in the next decade. This implies two things. No one digs up a major urban road in a developed city without obtaining a map of the underground infra-structure that they are likely to encounter. No one digs up an urban street without deploying the plant and manpower to achieve the dig. One of the difficulties of extending urban tree planting is the danger of interfering with the existing infrastructure of drains, gas, electricity, and communications. The other is the cost of digging and finishing the tree pits. Yet whenever they disturb the street, utility companies are armed with both maps and plant.

My plan is this, that for every twenty meters of road or pavement dug up whilst fixing breakdowns or installing upgraded pipe work, the utility company should be require to dig a tree pit. The citizenry, the voluntary sector, even the local administration should then find the tree and its sustenance. It would cost little and produce a trade off between the urban disruption of infra-structural maintenance or renewal and the arrival of more trees. Trees that improve both the aesthetic and the carbon emission absorbing qualities of the neighbourhood.

My hope is that in experiencing the beauty of the trees in these pages, more people will be stirred to fight to sustain and increase the trees in our world. What better memorial could any human wish, than to be remembered for planting a tree that long survives their own passing? For now, this book is about lives, very special lives, the lives of trees. Enjoy!

Jon Snow

When I first saw the Joshua trees in the Californian desert, their bristly beauty took me aback. They were twisted into such bizarre shapes, each with its own character, formed by the environmental struggle of growing out of dry soil.
As the first settlers arrived in California, after their exhausting journey, they mistook the trees for human figures in the distance. Seemingly welcoming them with outstretched arms, the trees were given the name 'Joshua', *in the bible the one who led the Israelites to the Promised Land.*
I certainly felt a similar affiliation with these trees, even though having seen pictures of them nothing can prepare one for the feeling of standing amongst a whole colony of Joshua trees.
I suddenly had an overwhelming sense of respect for trees, not only are they the lungs of nature, providing us with oxygen and cleaner air.
It is also their inner strength, surviving and adapting to often challenging environmental circumstances, which commands our admiration.
Pollution and the climate can all present threats to trees, however their resilience and self-healing and growing capabilities make them survive and even triumph over these challenges.
Thus they become social and political witnesses of our history and future through their resistance and longevity.

Throughout history trees and forests have been an important part of human existence. They have featured in literature from the Old Testament, the symbolic Apple tree in the Garden of Eden, Noah and the Olive leaf, to the plays of Shakespeare, the poetry of Hesse and countless other writers.
Trees in any shape or form can carry memories for us. The first kiss under a cherry blossom tree or making the tree our protector by hiding from ones parents after having been told off.
In Africa a tree has the great importance of giving shade, but also for providing a gathering space in a village. A place to witness stories being told beneath it, in the cool of the evening by the village elders.
Their global importance is recognised and more respected today.
Deforestation with its harrowing effects has spurred on new tree planting projects, the use of faster growing trees for the furniture industry has increased and recycling paper is widely practiced in the western world.
People's feelings and associations with trees are generally positive and respectful. Trees embody life, they show us the seasons in a city landscape, and they provide us with wood, food and shelter. Their silence demands our respect.
'It is difficult to place a monetary value on the many vital services that trees provide. However, the California Department of Forestry and Fire Protection calculates that a single tree that lives for fifty years will contribute service worth nearly $200,000 (in 1994 dollars) to the community during its lifetime. This includes providing oxygen ($31,250), recycling water and regulating humidity ($37,000), controlling air pollution ($62,500), producing protein ($2,500), providing shelter for wildlife ($31,250), and controlling land erosion and fertilizing the soil ($31,250).

These photographs show the struggles and the victories of trees throughout their lifecycle in all kinds of habitats.
This collection includes a variety of trees inhabiting Britain, California, Cuba, Germany and Spain. Even though these are very diverse countries, their trees experience similar challenges. They all are reliant on their climate.
Exposure to extreme weather conditions and climates will have an effect on their growth. Global warming caused by carbon dioxide pollution has a direct result on the climate and nature.

There are also interesting political and social issues, which are affecting trees well- being. Remarkably, a very poor country like Cuba is still planting trees in containers in a very run down neighbourhood in Havana. Additionally, outside Havana, old trees have been respectfully incorporated into the design of a building on the grounds of an old sugar mill.
On the other hand, the rich state of California could not prevent the damage caused by the careless behaviour of one human, resulting into huge fires in the summer of 2003, with devastating consequences. Even more recently torrential rain caused huge mudslides on Haiti, drowning villages and their inhabitants, as most of the island had been deforested.

In this book are trees challenged by their climate and soil conditions. Old survivors such as the 4000year old Yew trees in Kingsley Vale, and transformed trees, which have changed shape or colour due to outside influences. In one example strong winds along the British coast are moulding the tree's branches into seemingly one-sided hairstyles. The book also includes trees reclaiming their habitat i.e. taking over old greenhouses on a derelict farm. Finally we see trees participating in life and adapting to the habitat they have been given, shaping their landscape and at the same time being shaped by it.

With *The Whisper Of A Million Leaves* I am hoping to reinforce the feeling of respect for trees in the onlooker through my photography, and to awaken more interest and encourage a greater awareness for our environment and particularly for trees. Even though our attitude towards trees has improved, a lot more can be done for their conservation.
Paper recycling in England is still only 4% compared to other European country's 64%. Taking a proactive environmental attitude by recycling and buying paper and paper products from eco- efficient companies, who are sourcing raw materials from renewable forests, is a consumer's choice.

Strangely enough, one of my first childhood memories of a tree involved the highly poisonous 'Laburnum' tree.
I was about six when I gorged myself on its peapod like fruit. Half an hour later I was violently sick and rushed into hospital. Luckily it all happened very quickly and I survived.
Although not a happy memory, it is something I will never forget and it has left me with a profound respect for nature's powers and trees. *B.H.*

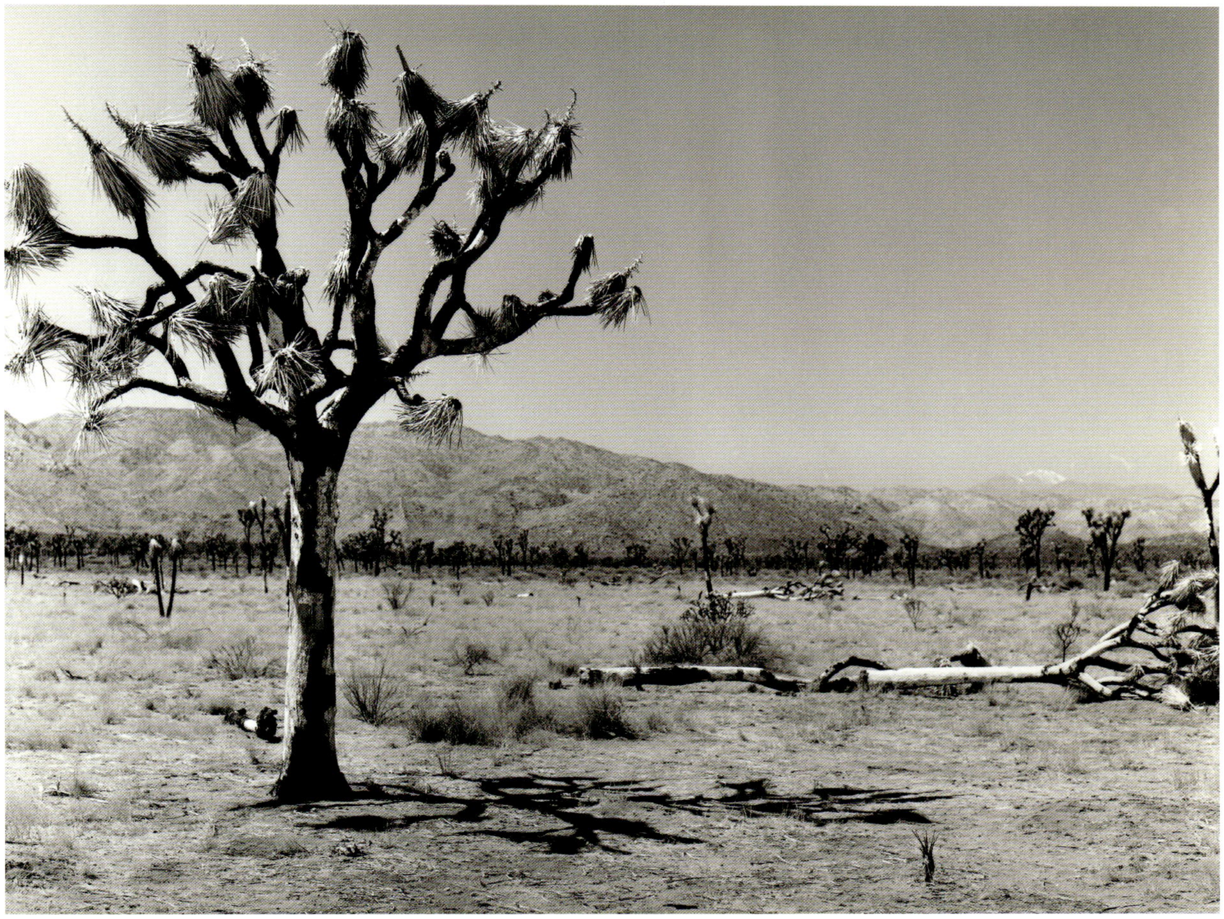

CHALLENGE

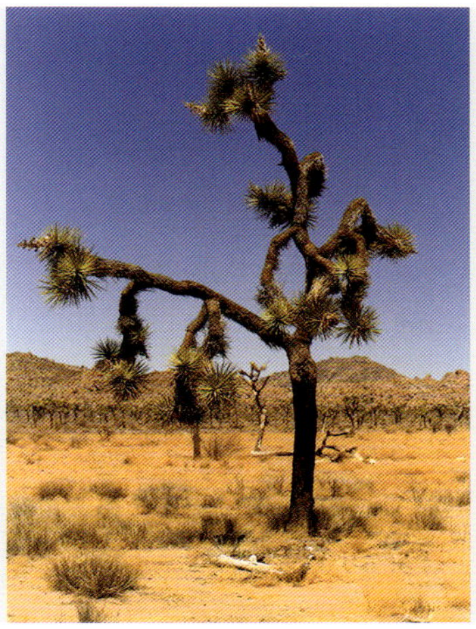

Give me land of boughs in leaf,
 A land of trees that stand;
Where trees are fallen there is grief;
I love no leafless land.

A.E.Housman, 1859-1936

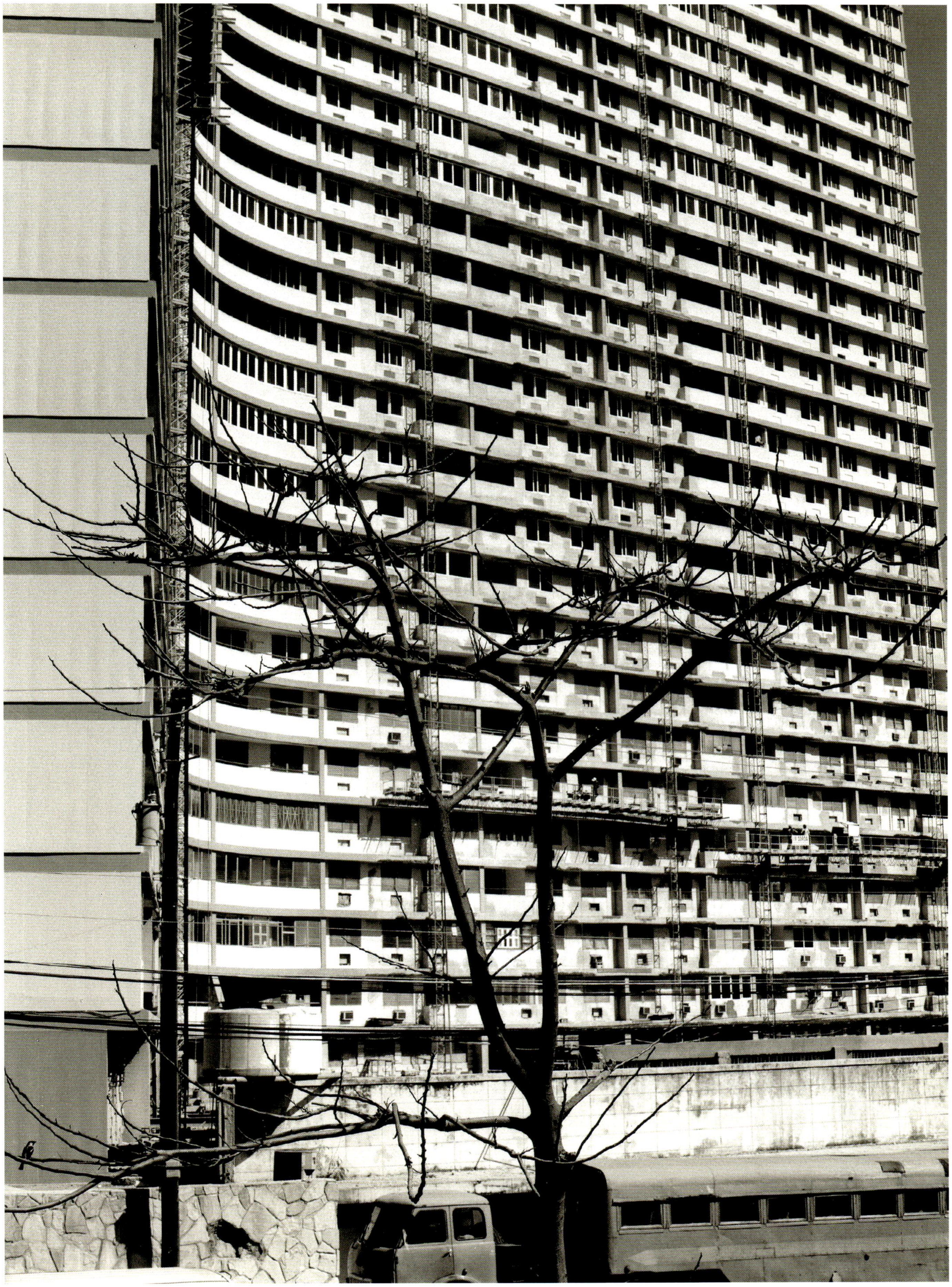

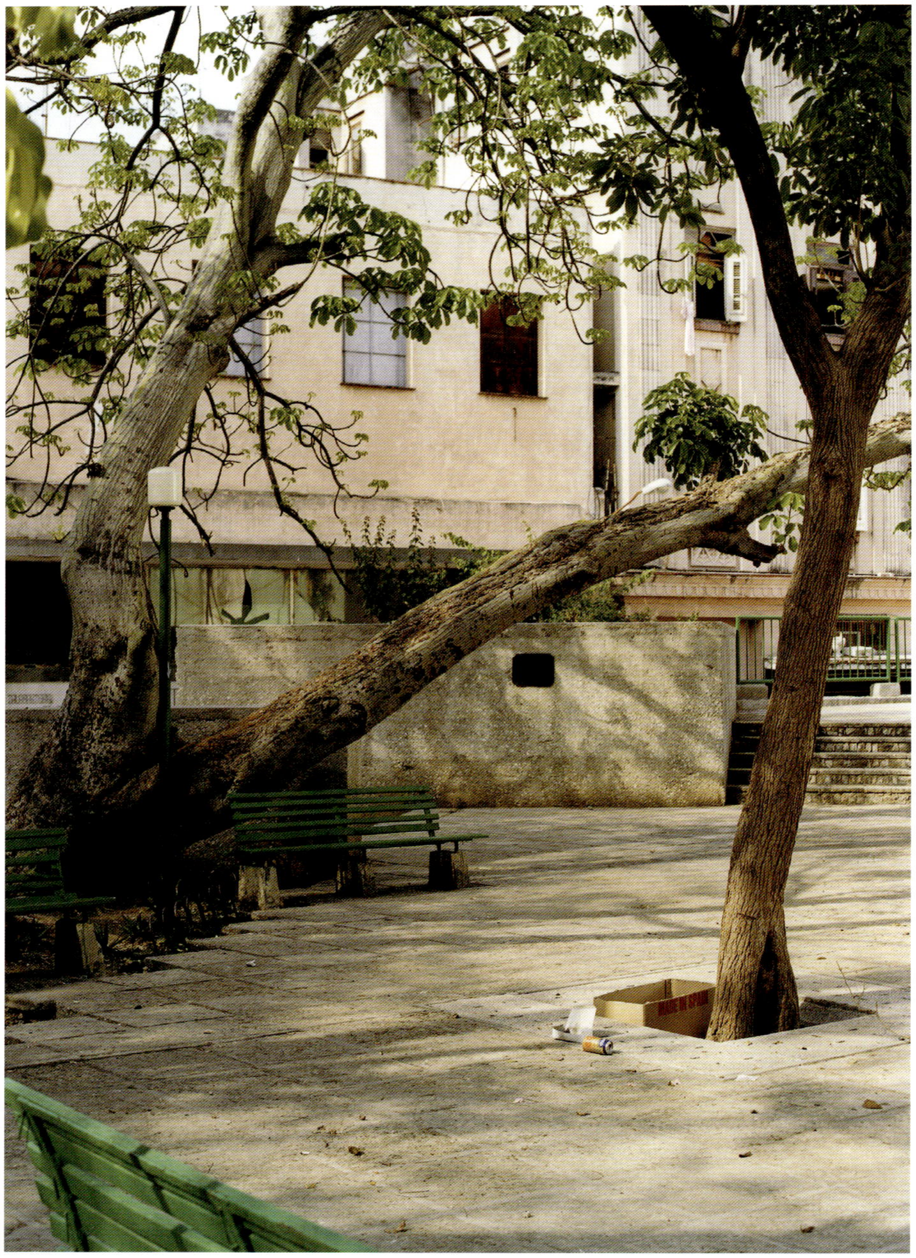

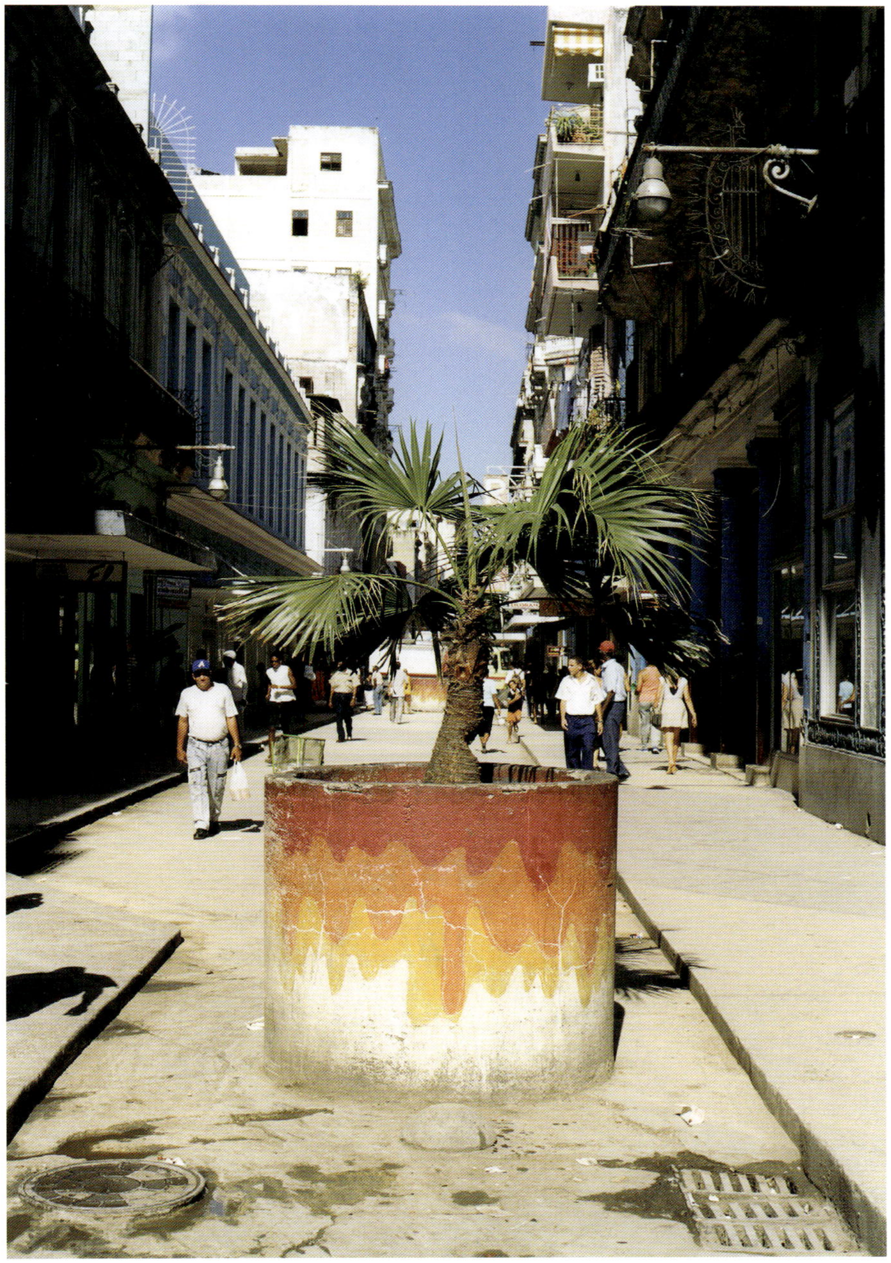

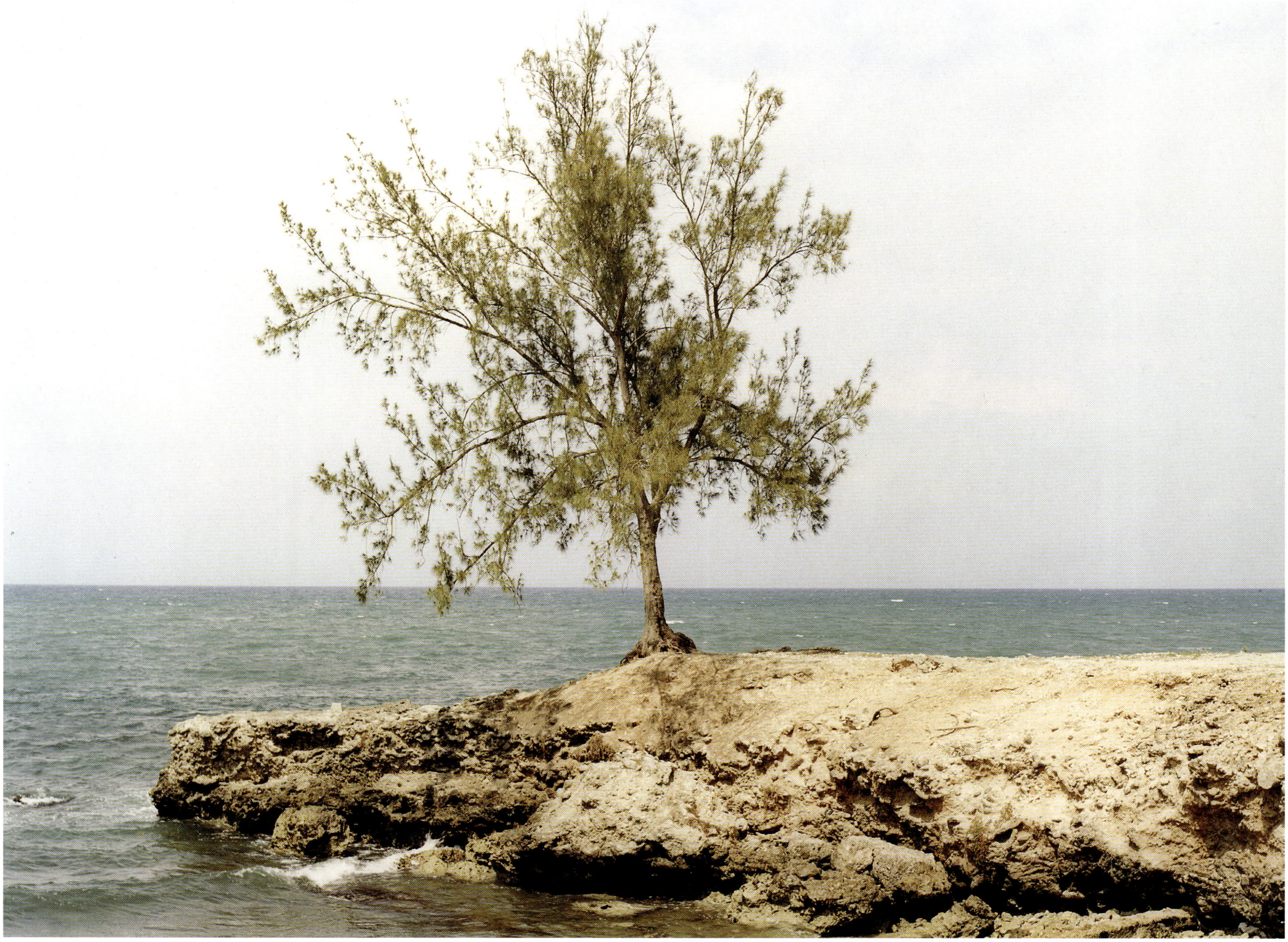

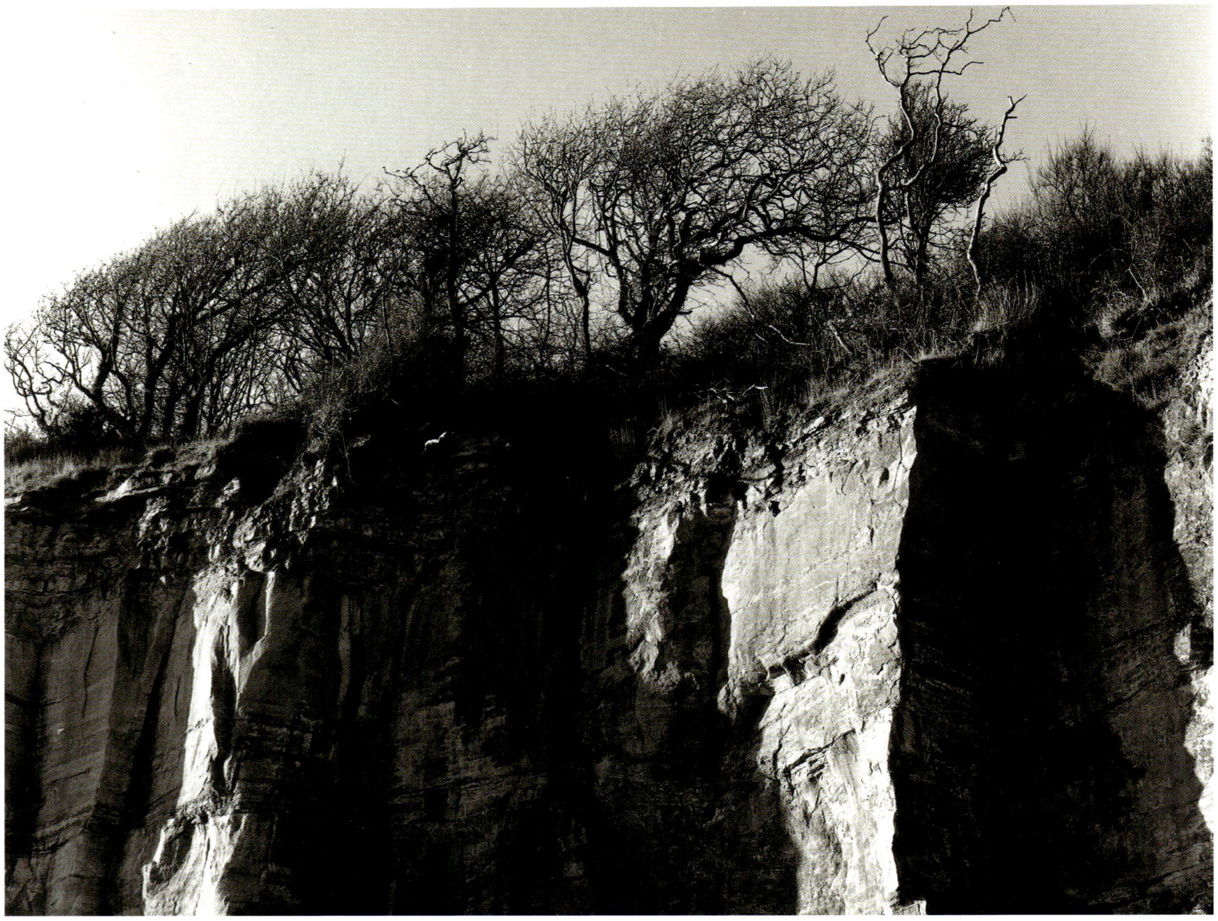

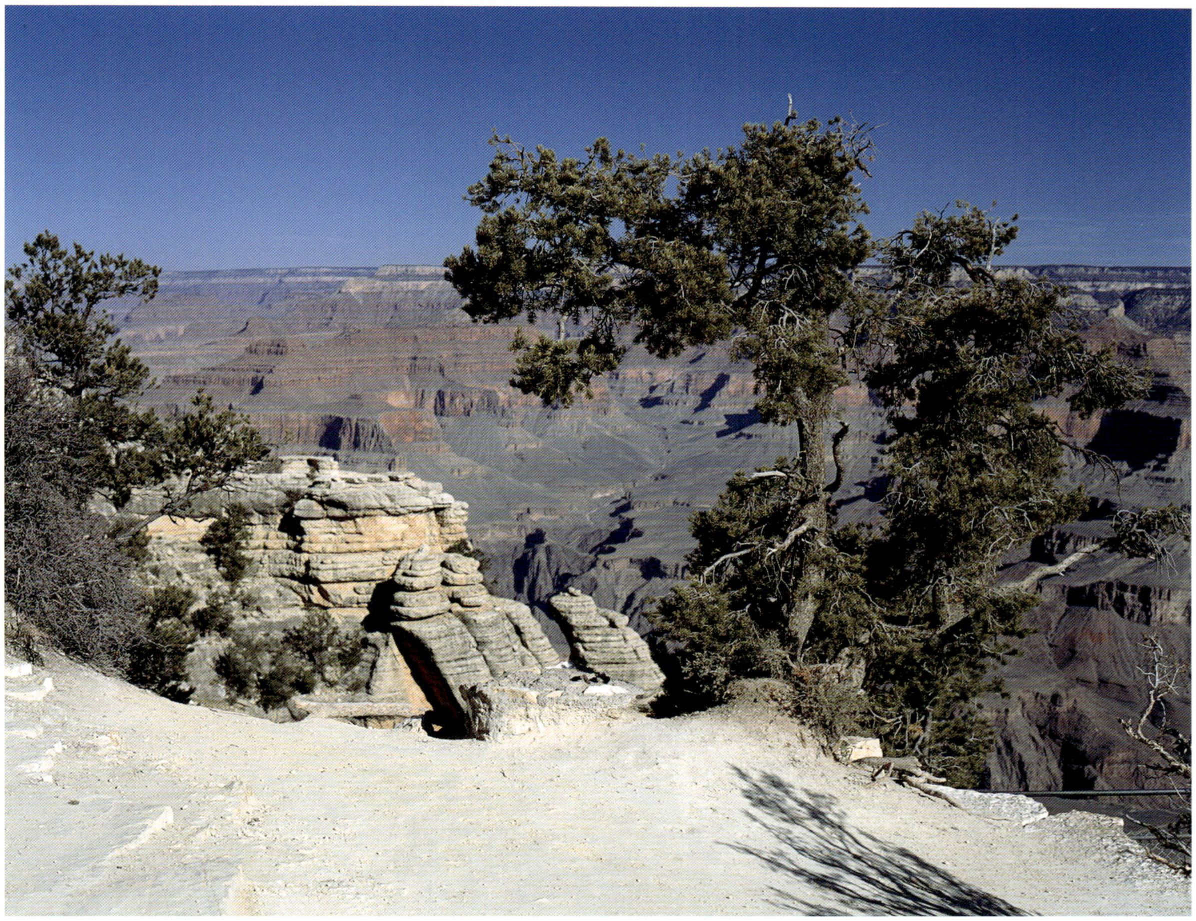

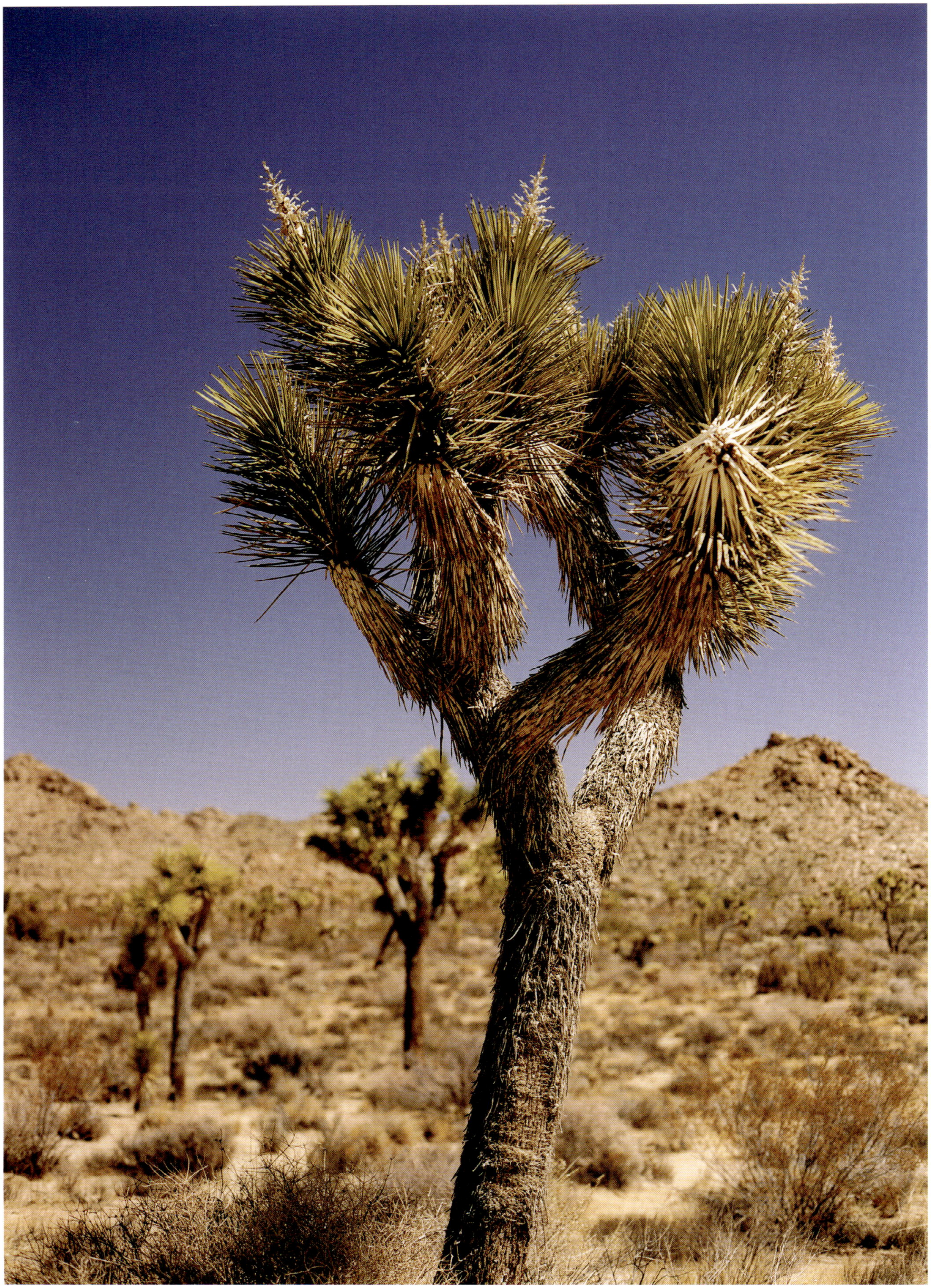

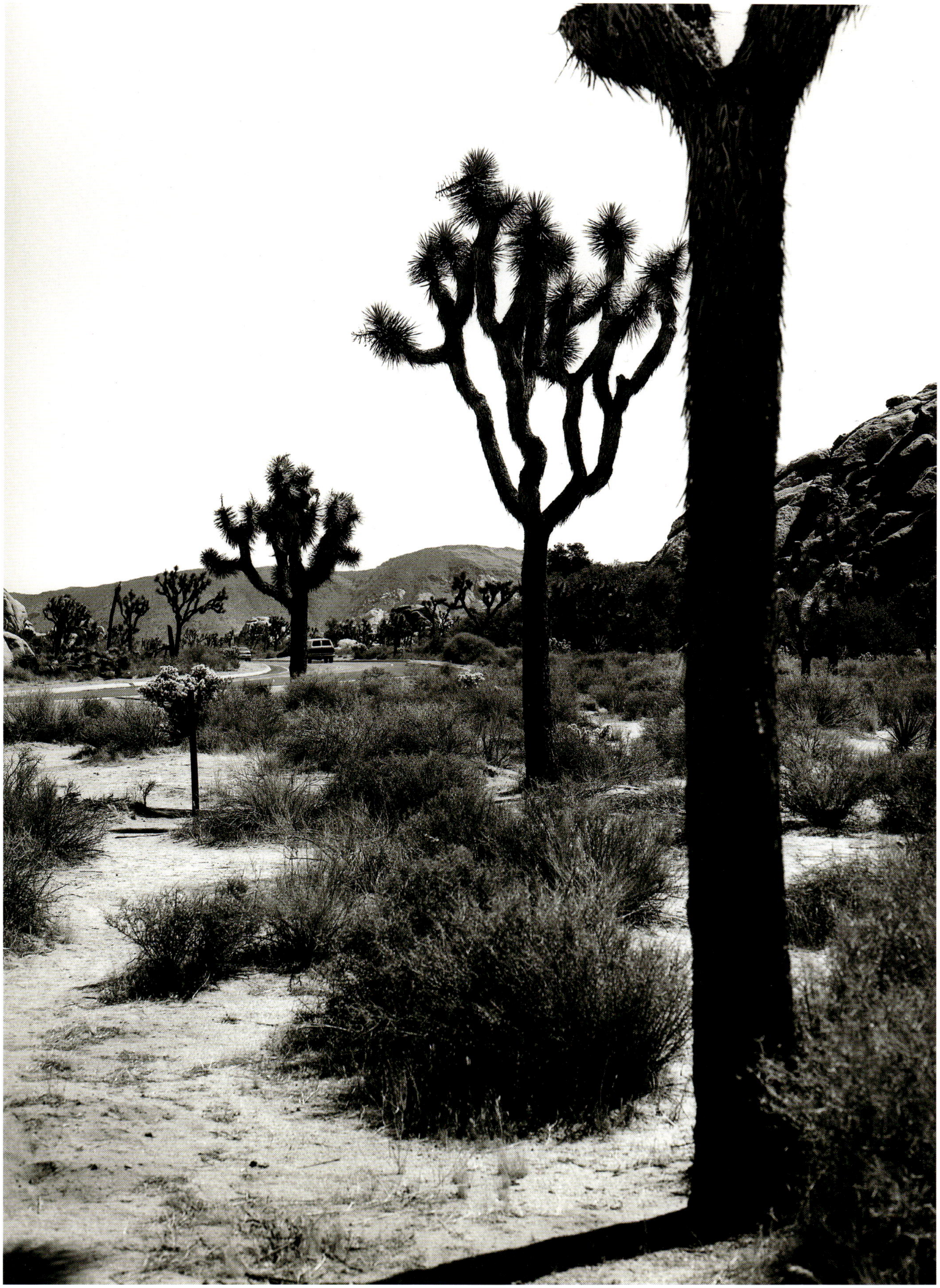

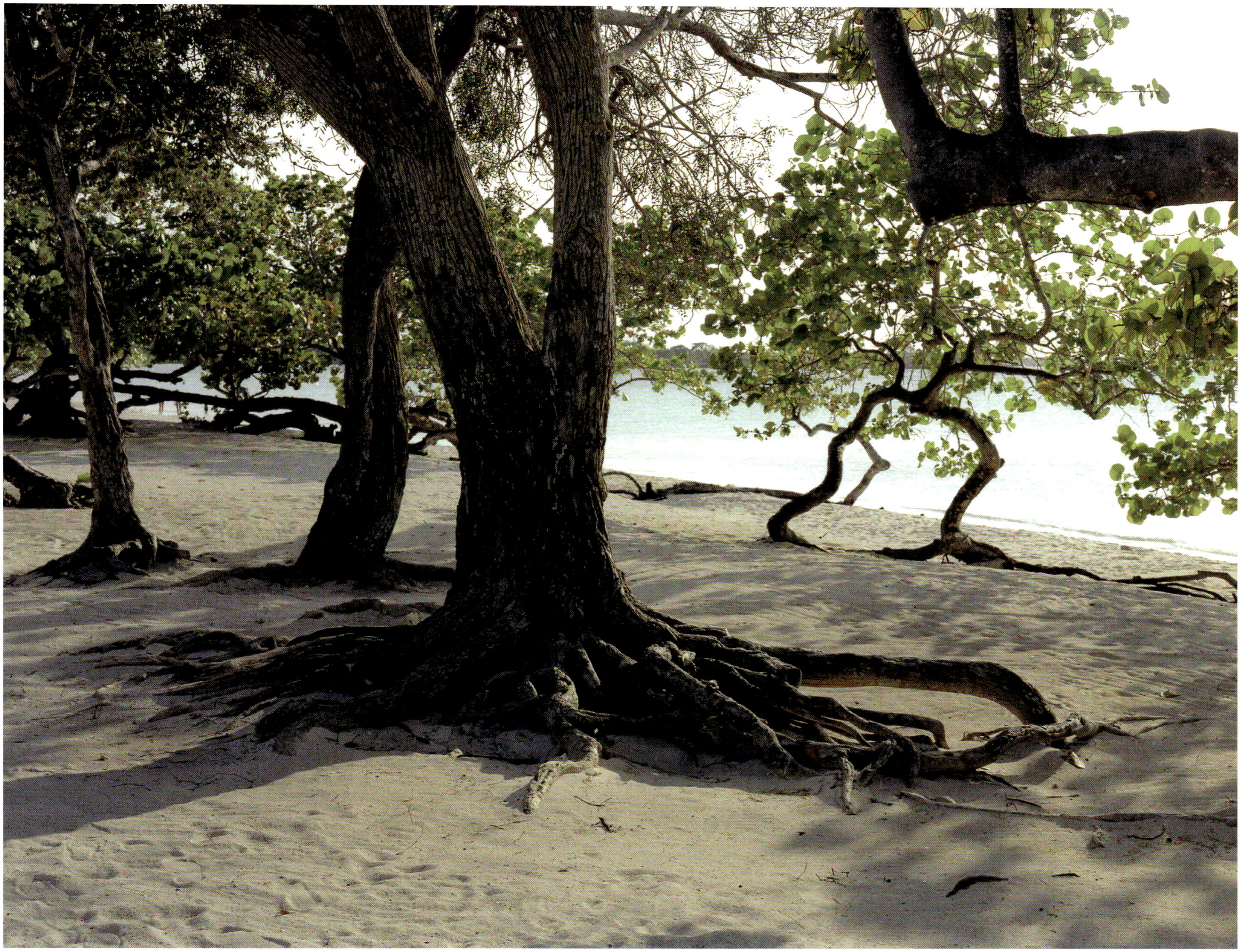

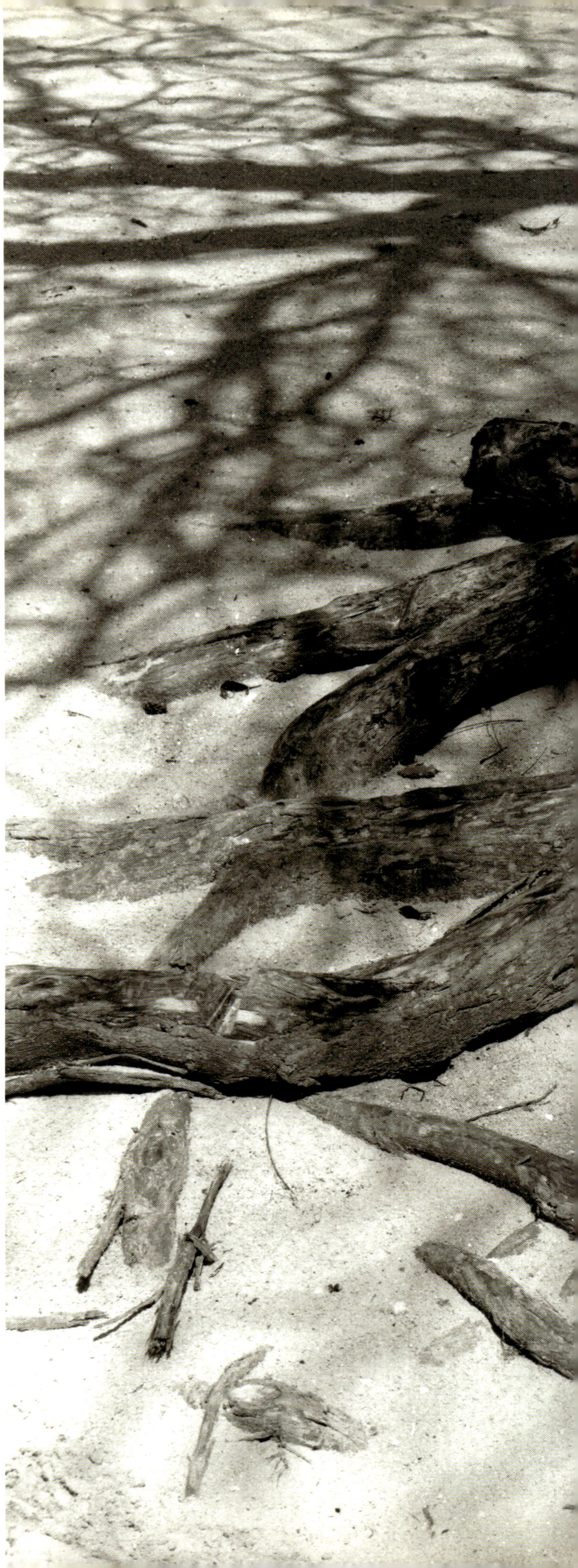

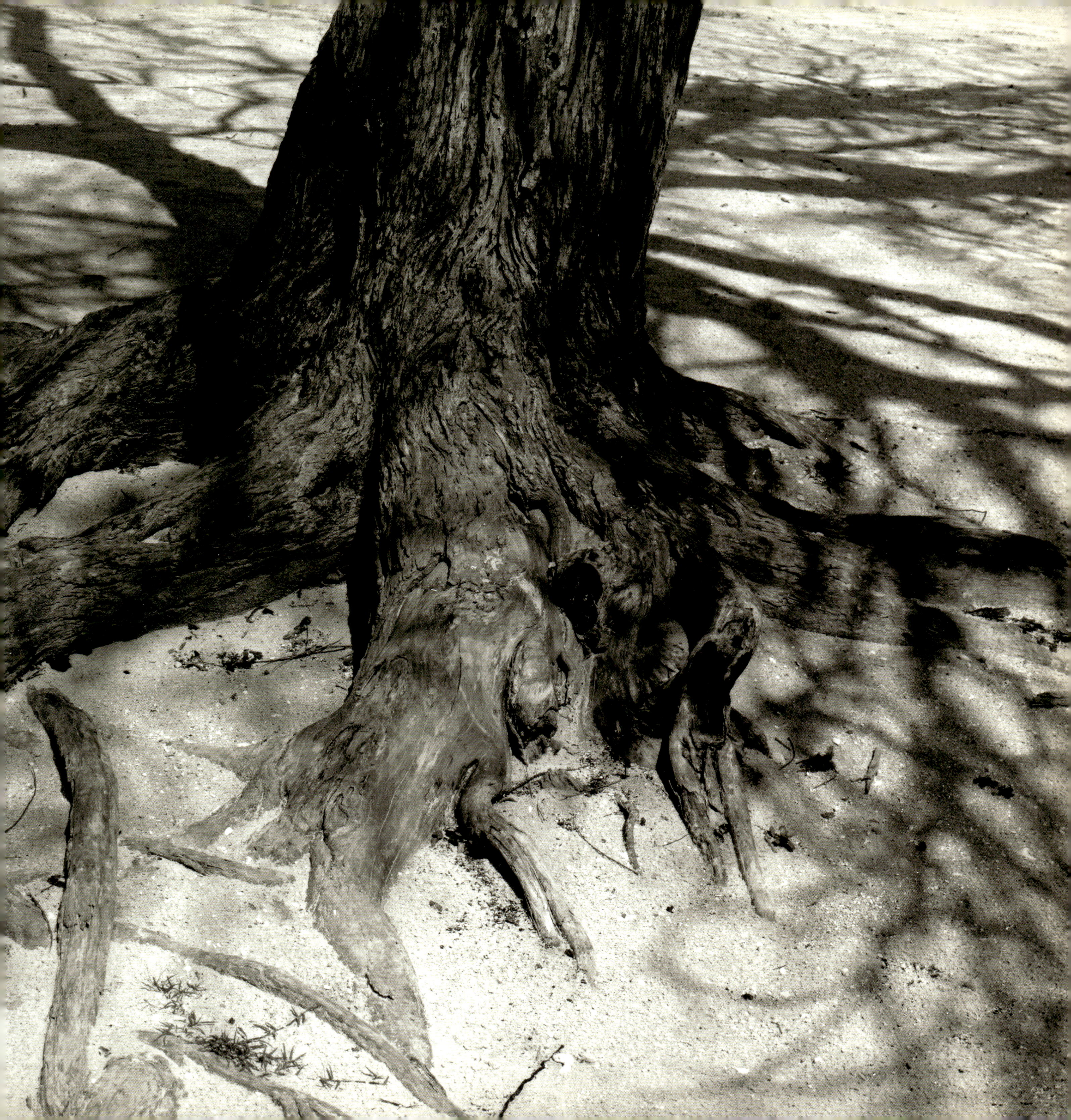

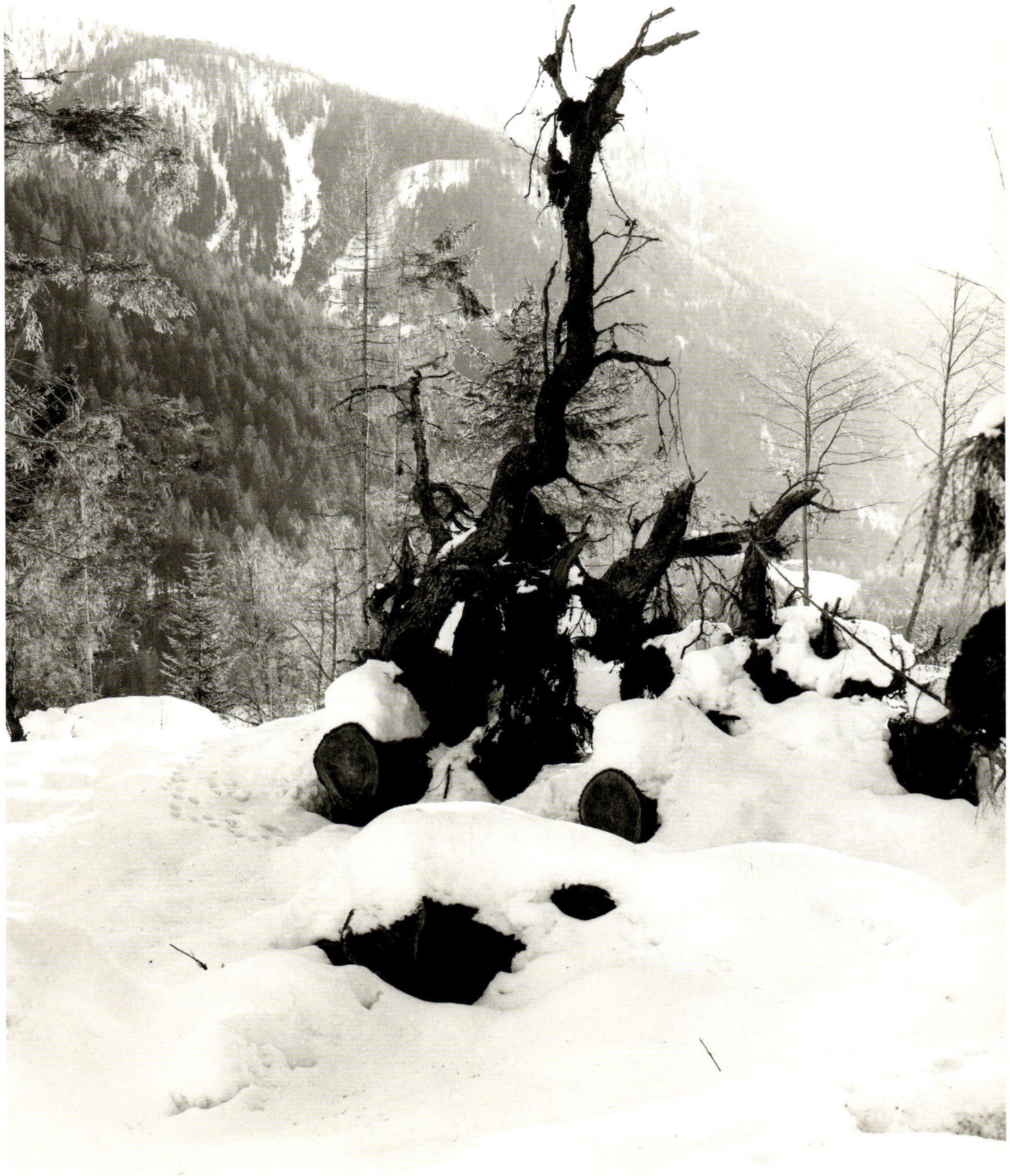

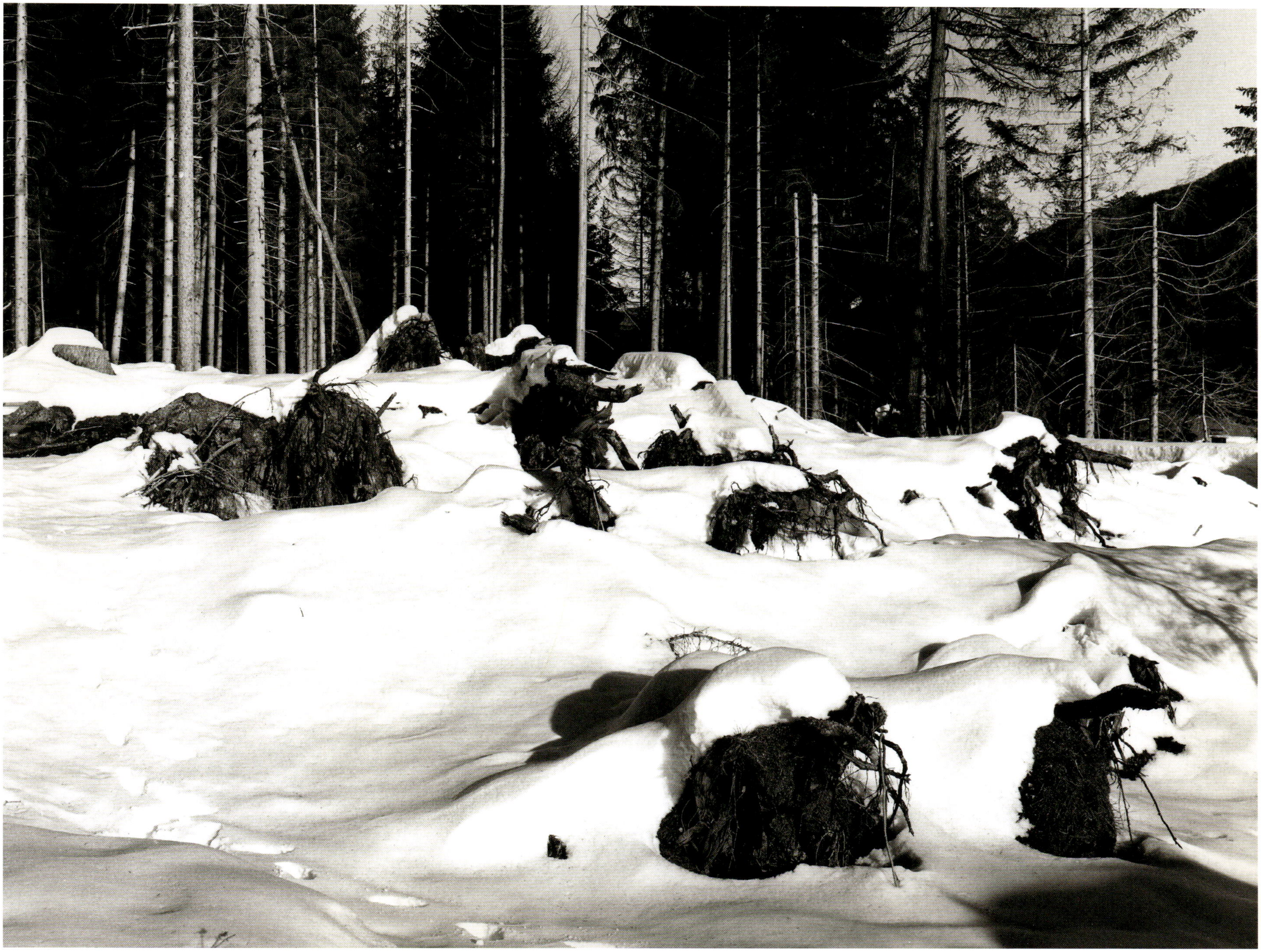

SURVIVAL

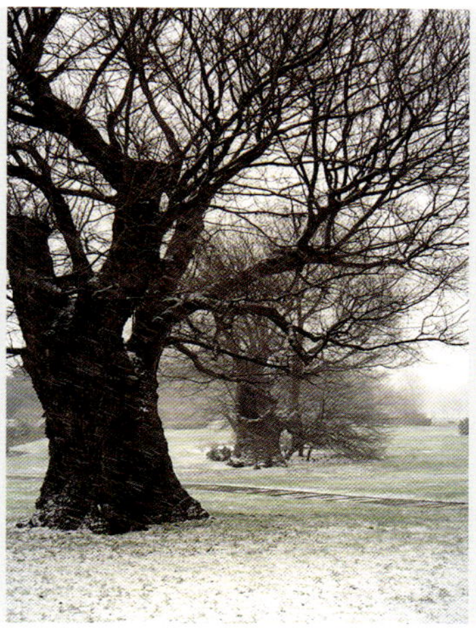

I like trees because they seem more resigned to the way they have to live than other things do.

Willa Cather, 1873-1947, O Pioneers

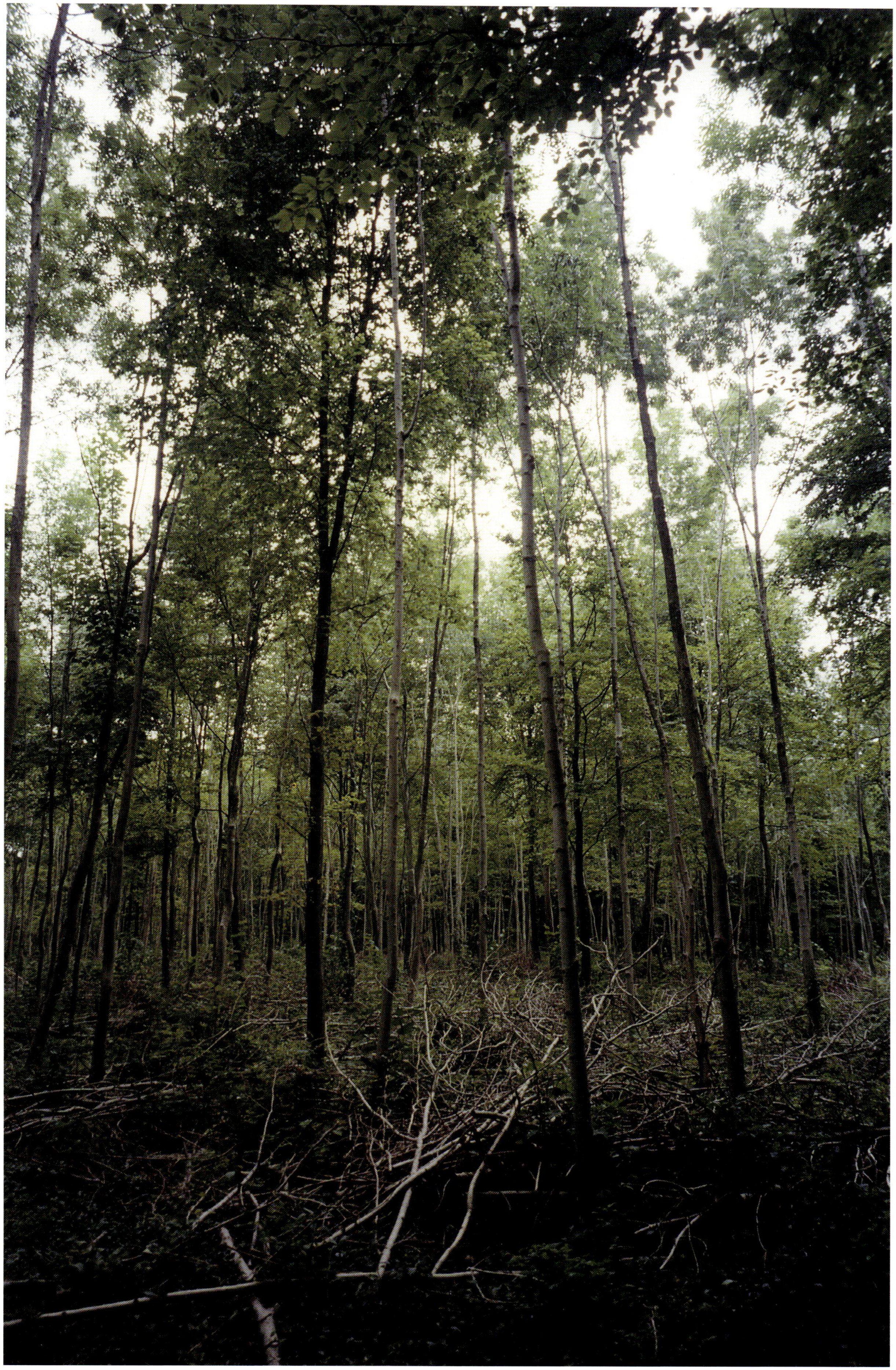

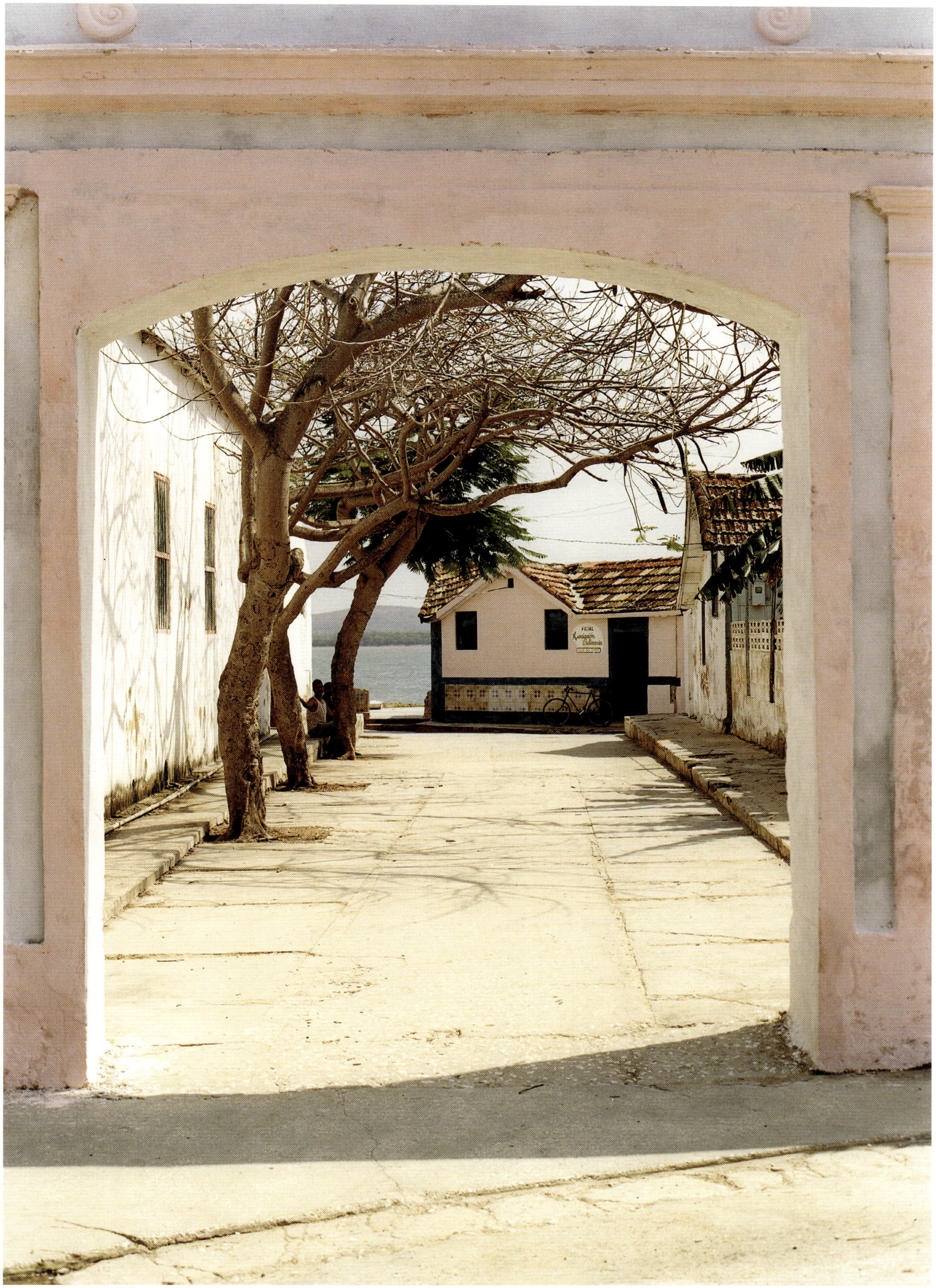

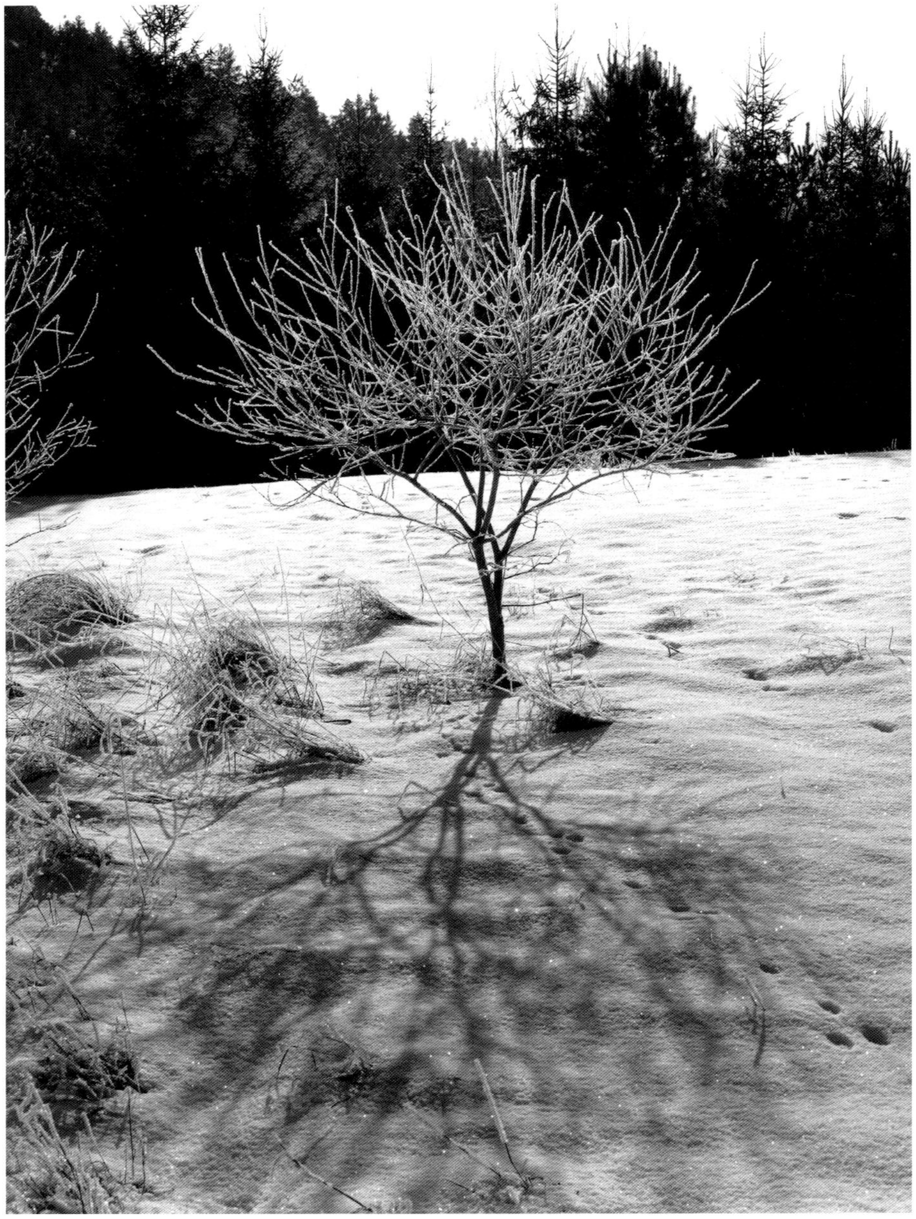

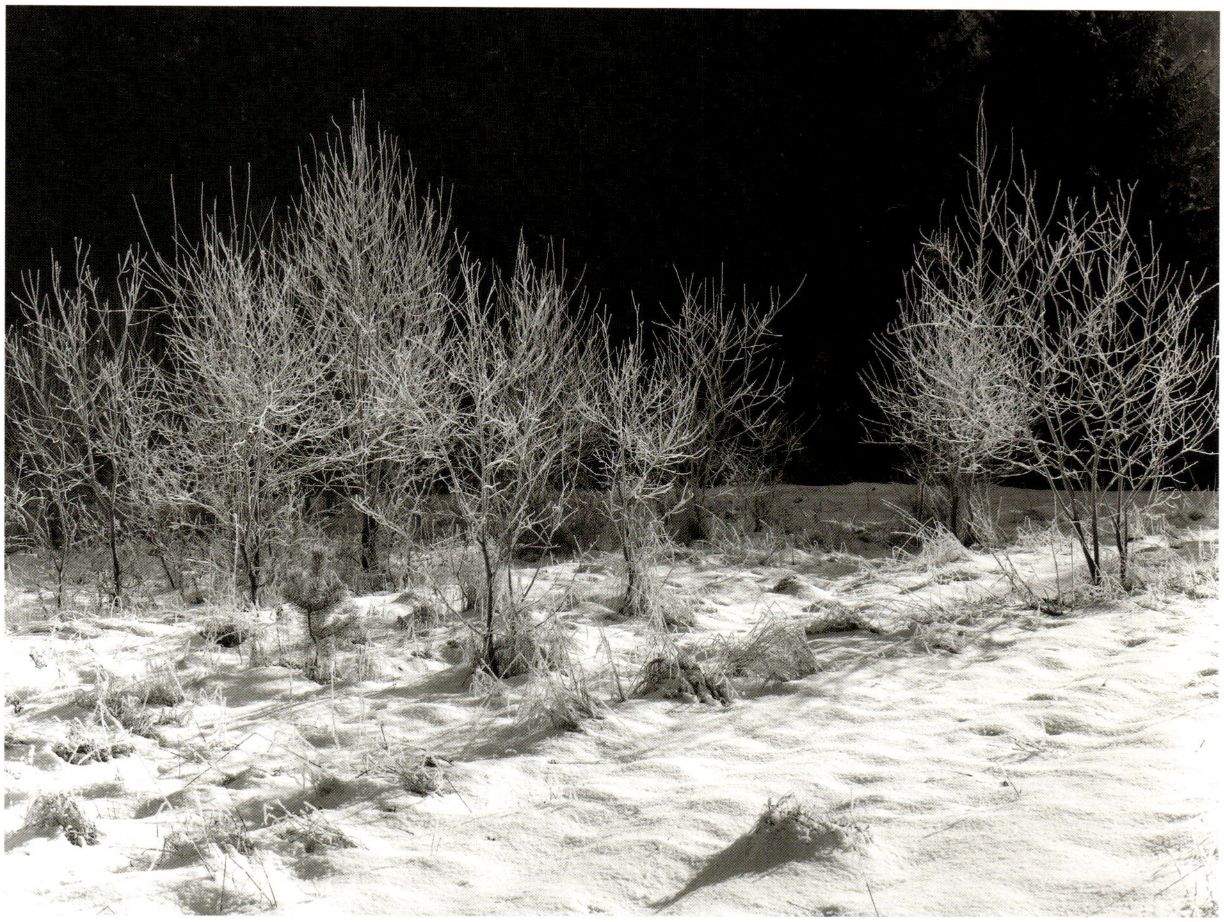

Because they are primeval,
Because they outlive us,
Because they are fixed,
Trees seem to emanate a sense of permanence,
And though rooted in earth,
They seem to touch the sky.
For these reasons it is natural to feel we might learn wisdom from them,
To haunt about them with the idea if we could only read
their silent riddle rightly we should learn some secret vital to our own lives;
Or even more specifically, some secret vital to our real,
Our lasting and spiritual existence.

Kim Taplin, Tongues in Trees, 1989

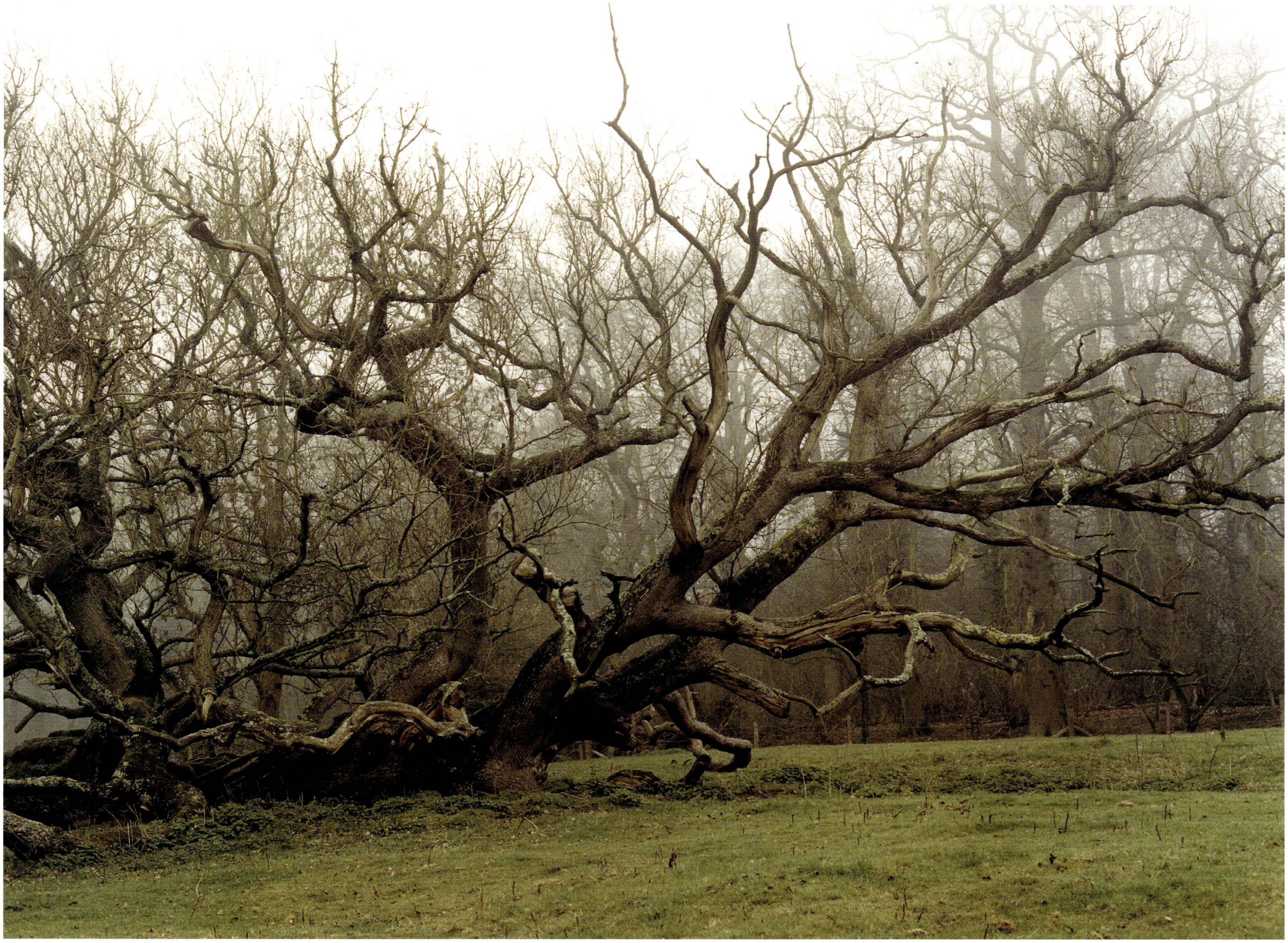

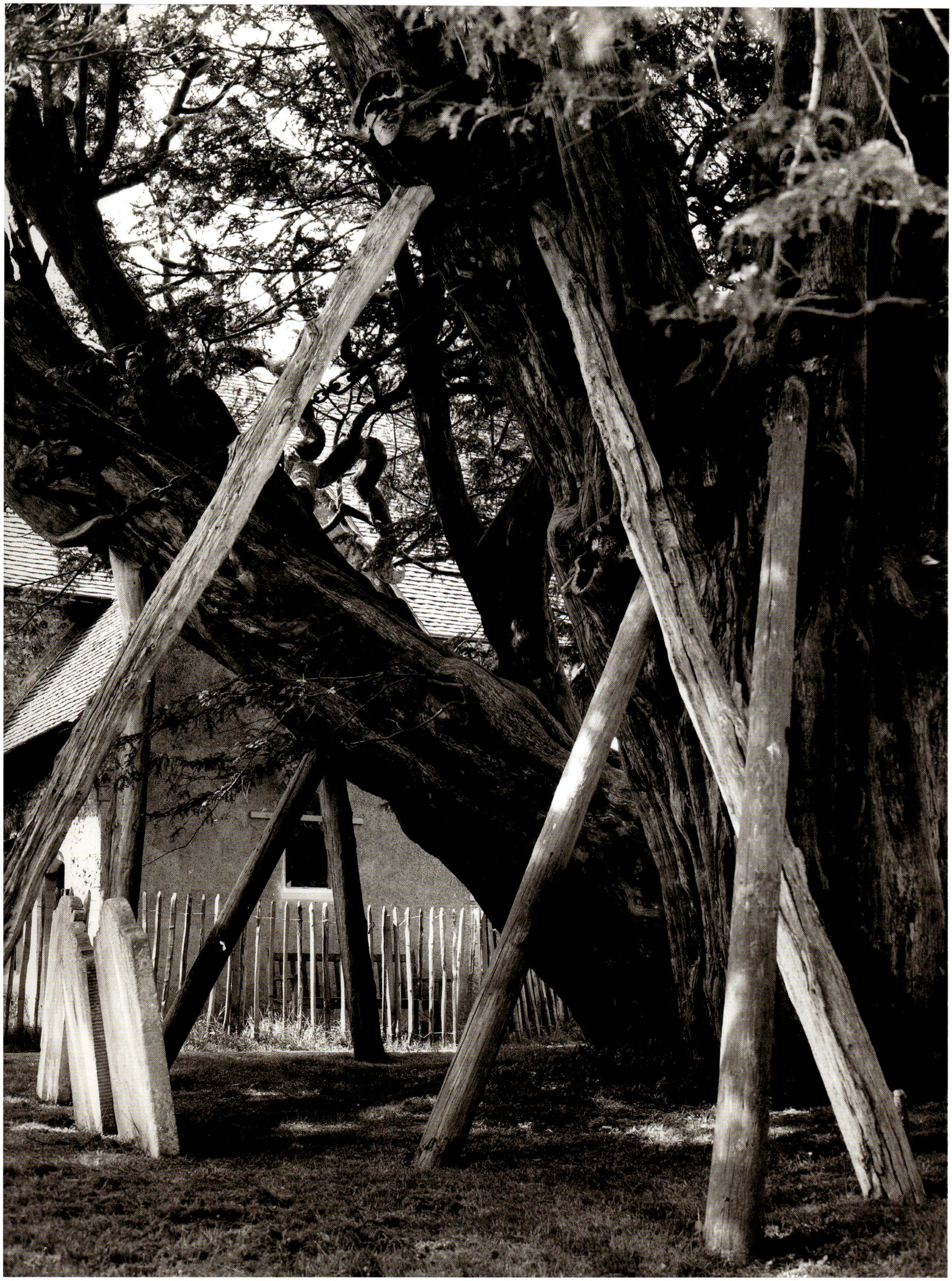

When you enter a grove peopled with ancient trees, higher than the ordinary,
and shutting out the sky with their thickly inter- twined branches,
do not the stately shadows of the wood, the stillness of the place,
and the awful gloom of this doomed cavern then strike you
with the presence of the deity?

Seneca, 4BC-65AD

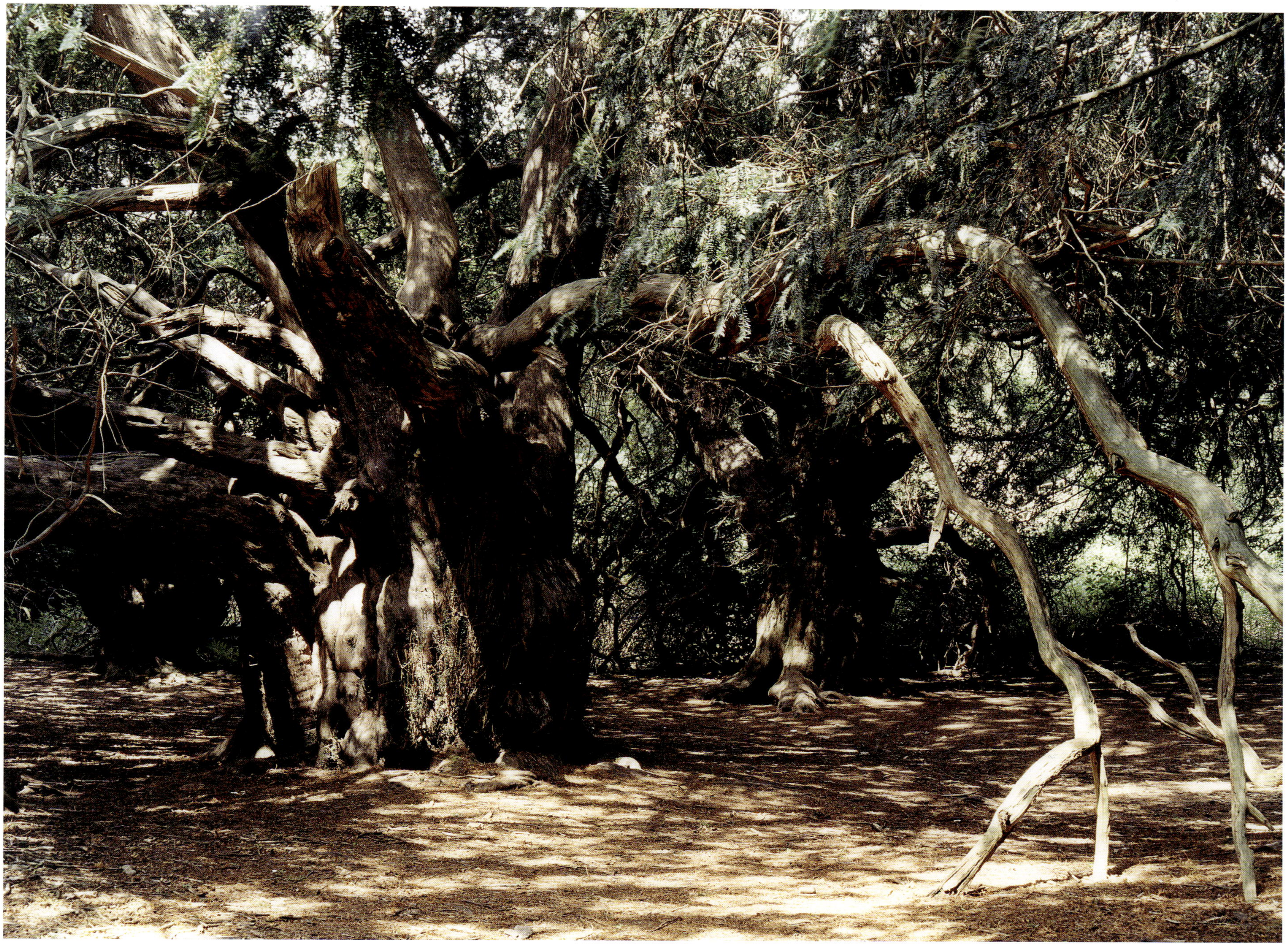

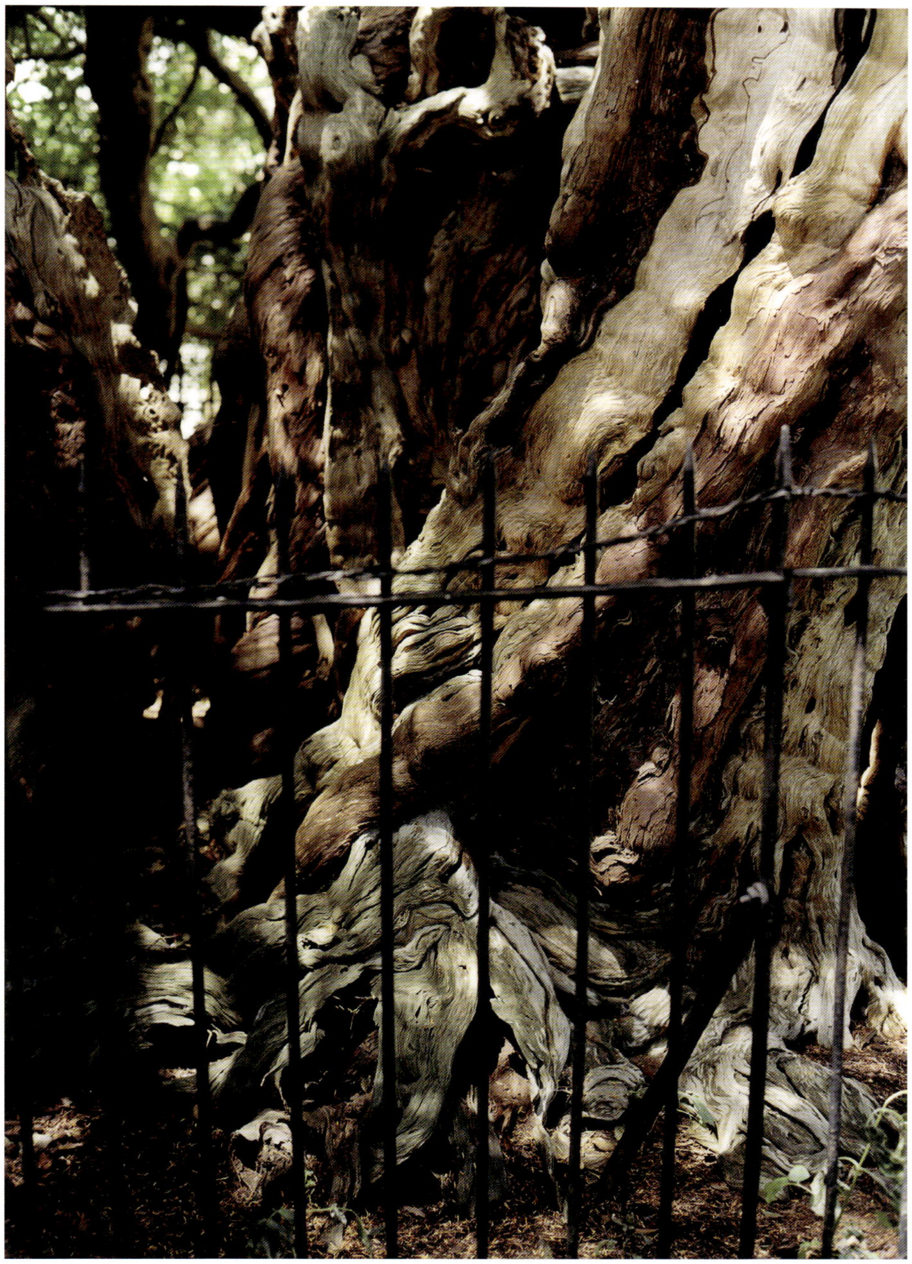

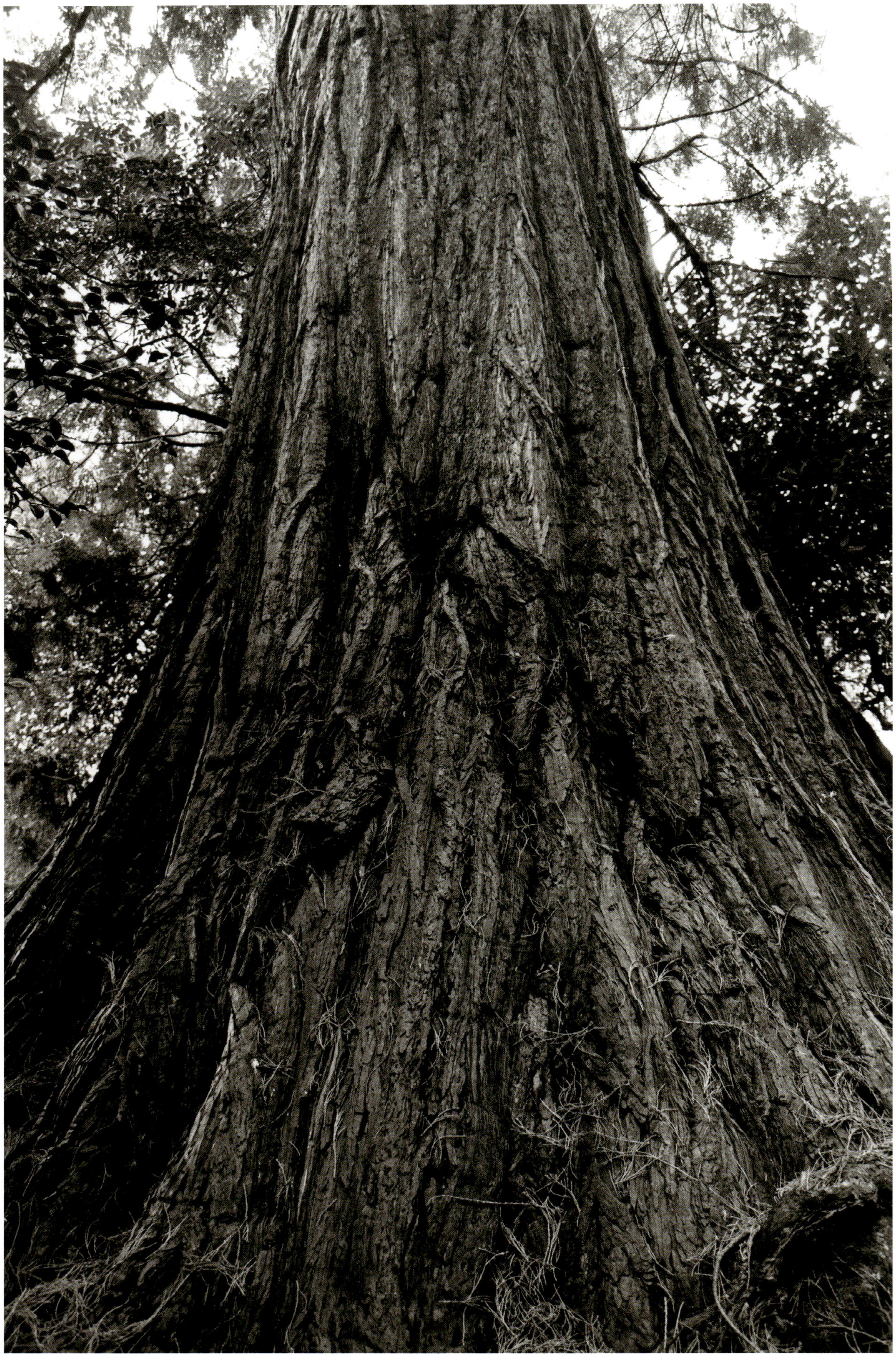

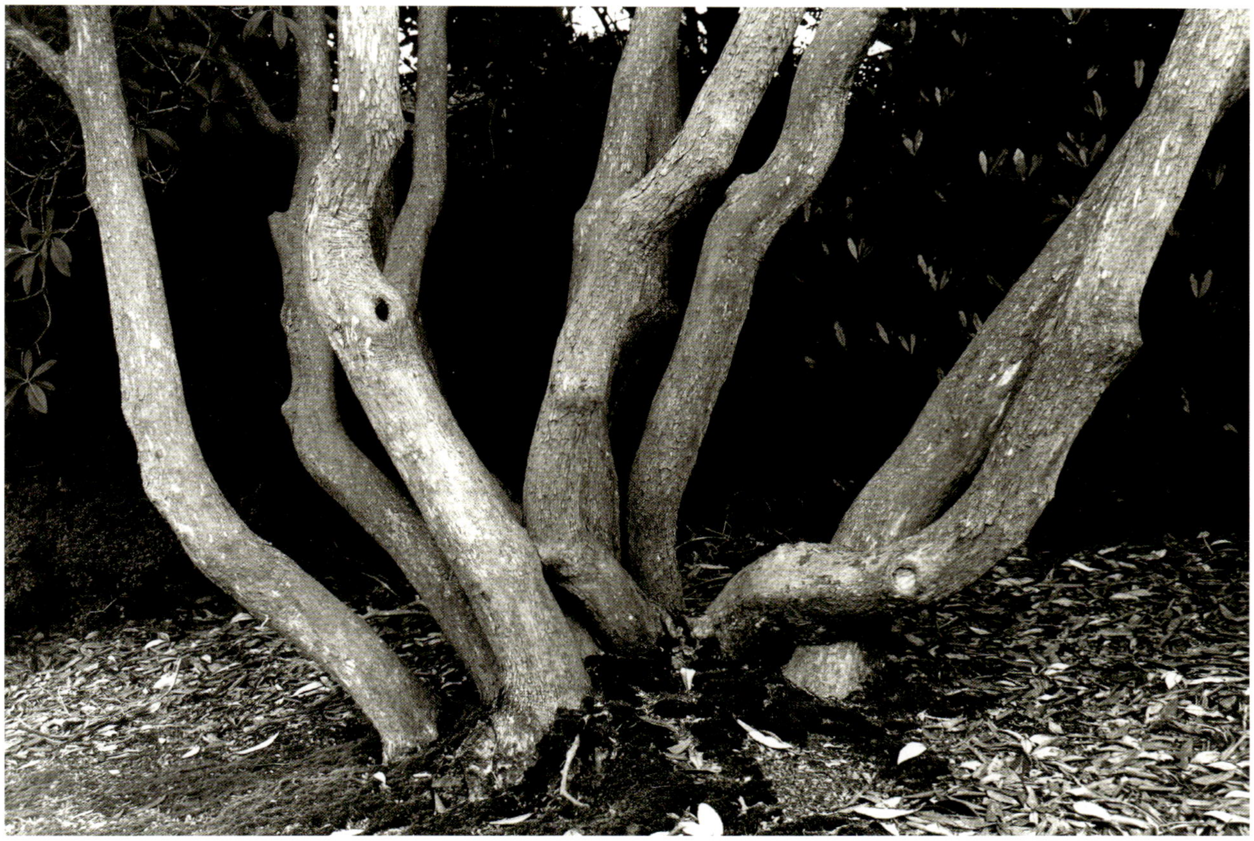

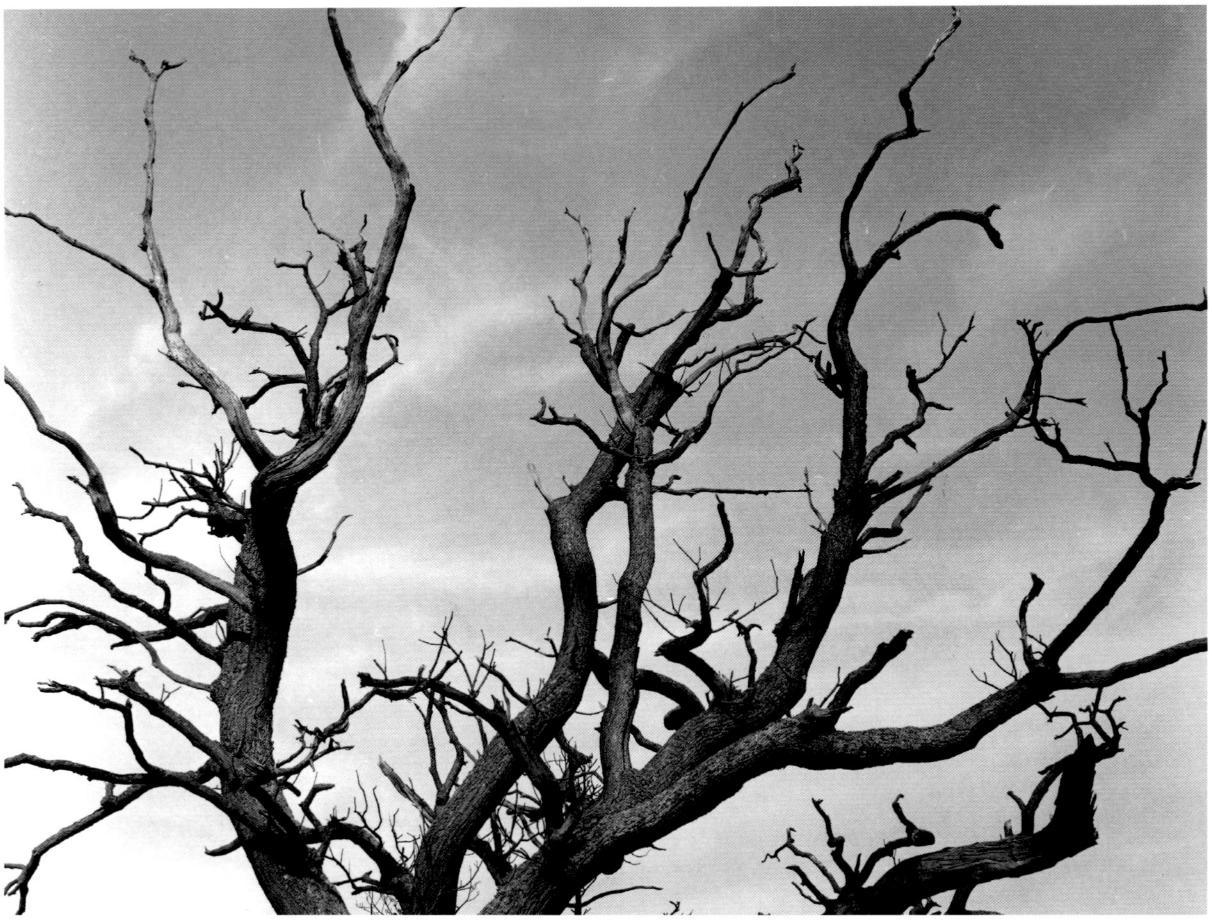

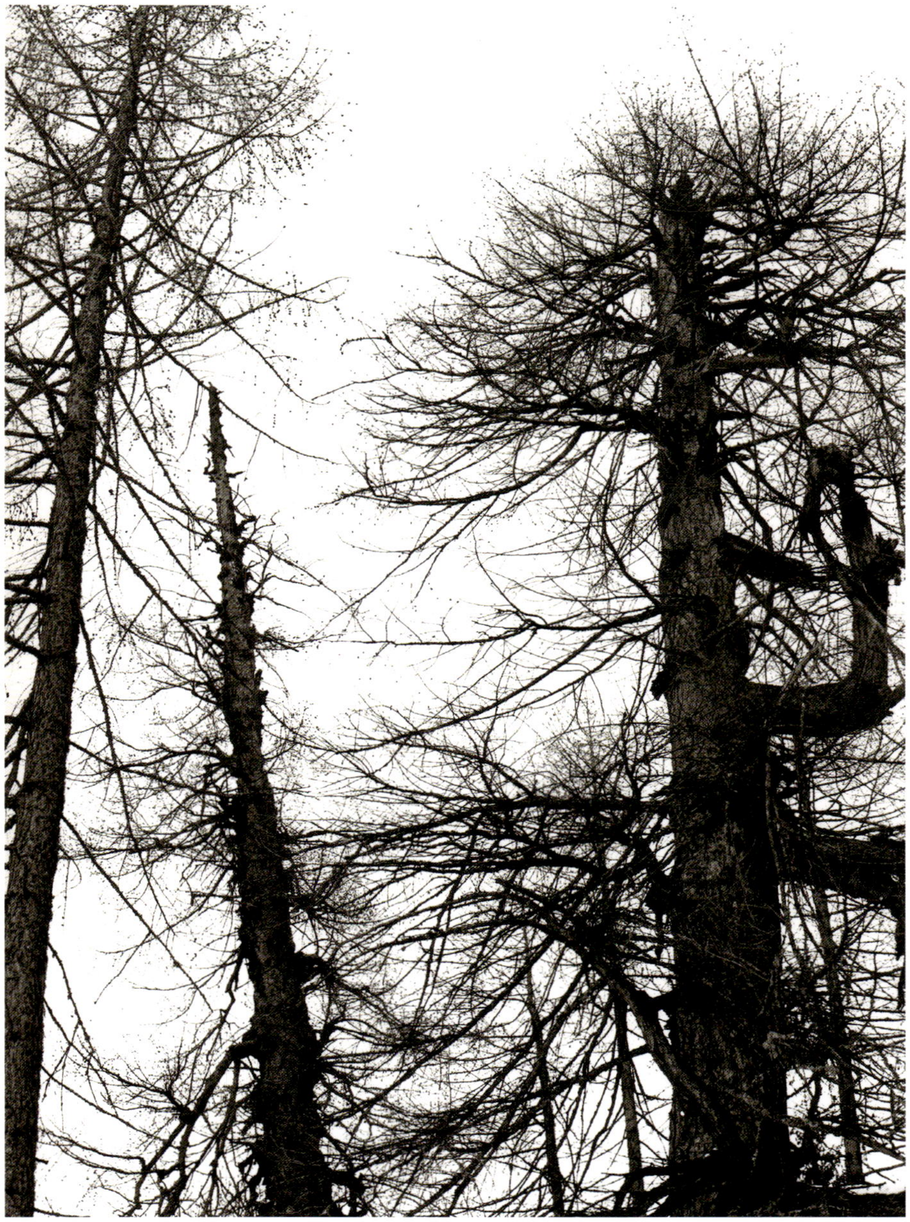

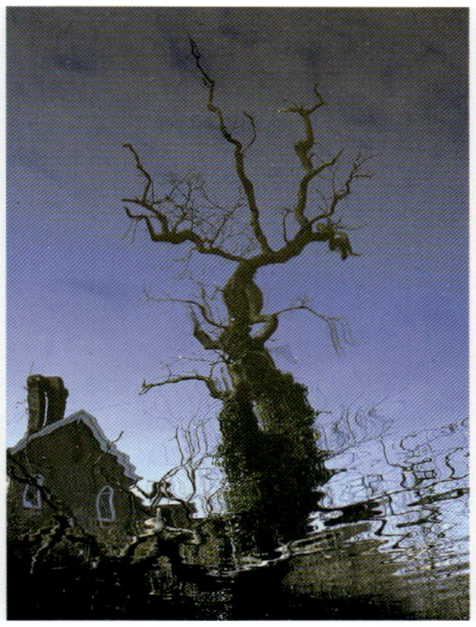

In towering splendor once I stood
A regal monarch of the wood,
My branches once reached to the sky
See me now but do not cry.
The creators work has yet to cease
I've become shelter for bird and beast,
And when at last I fall to Earth
The life I leave will inspire new birth;
A seedling springs forth from the ground
Nature's cycle goes round and round.

S. Edward Palmer, 1964, Spirit Tree

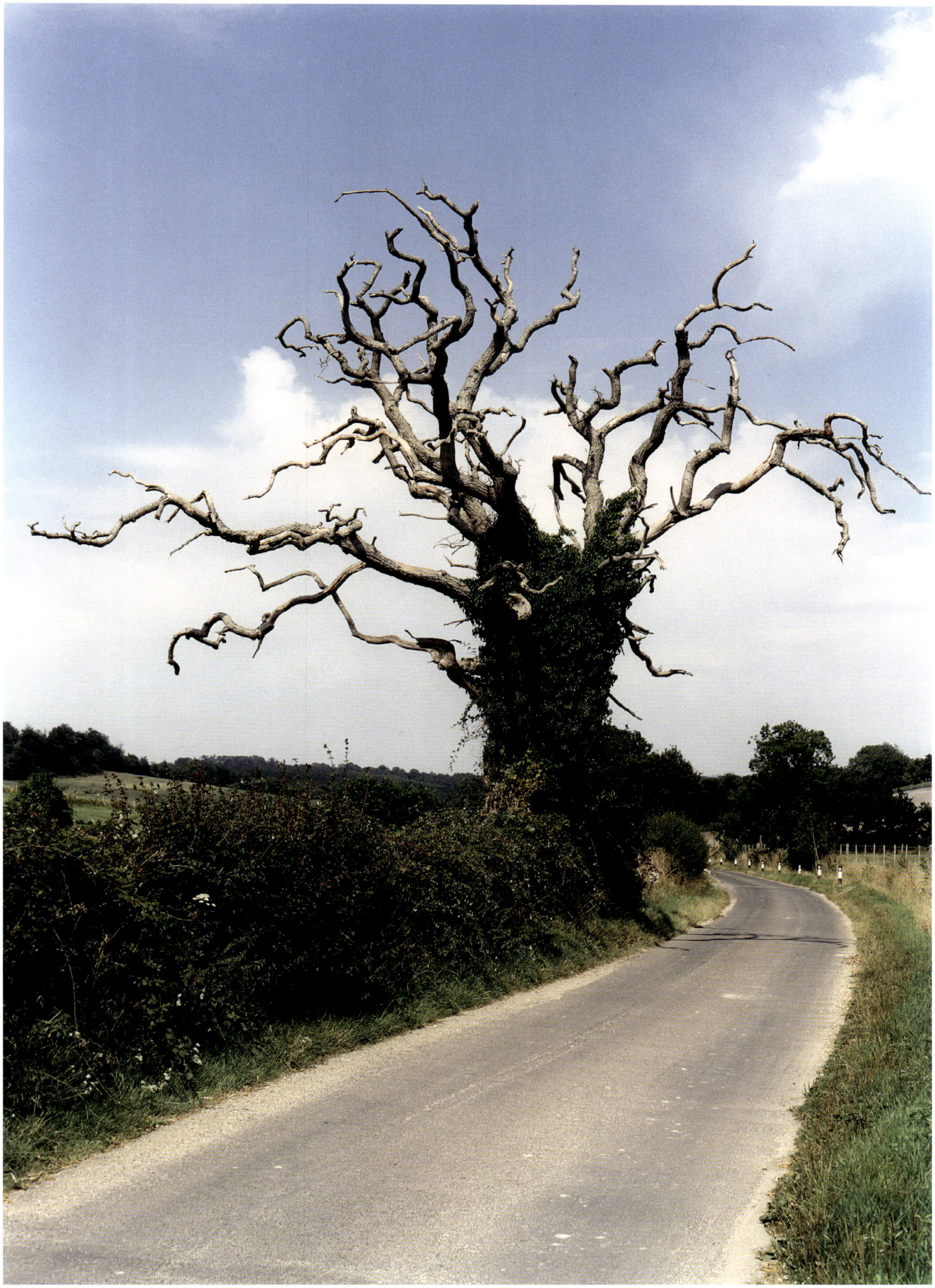

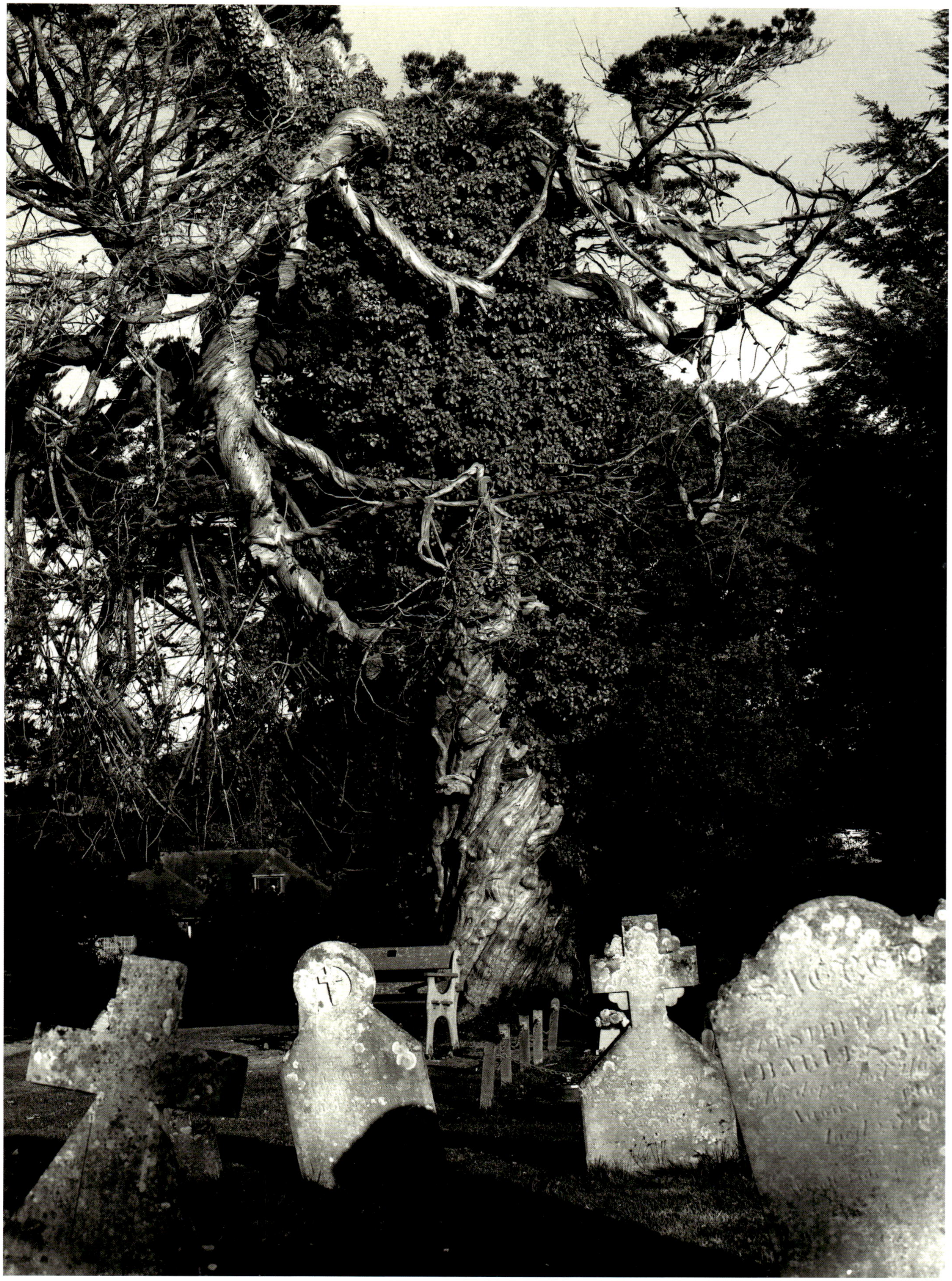

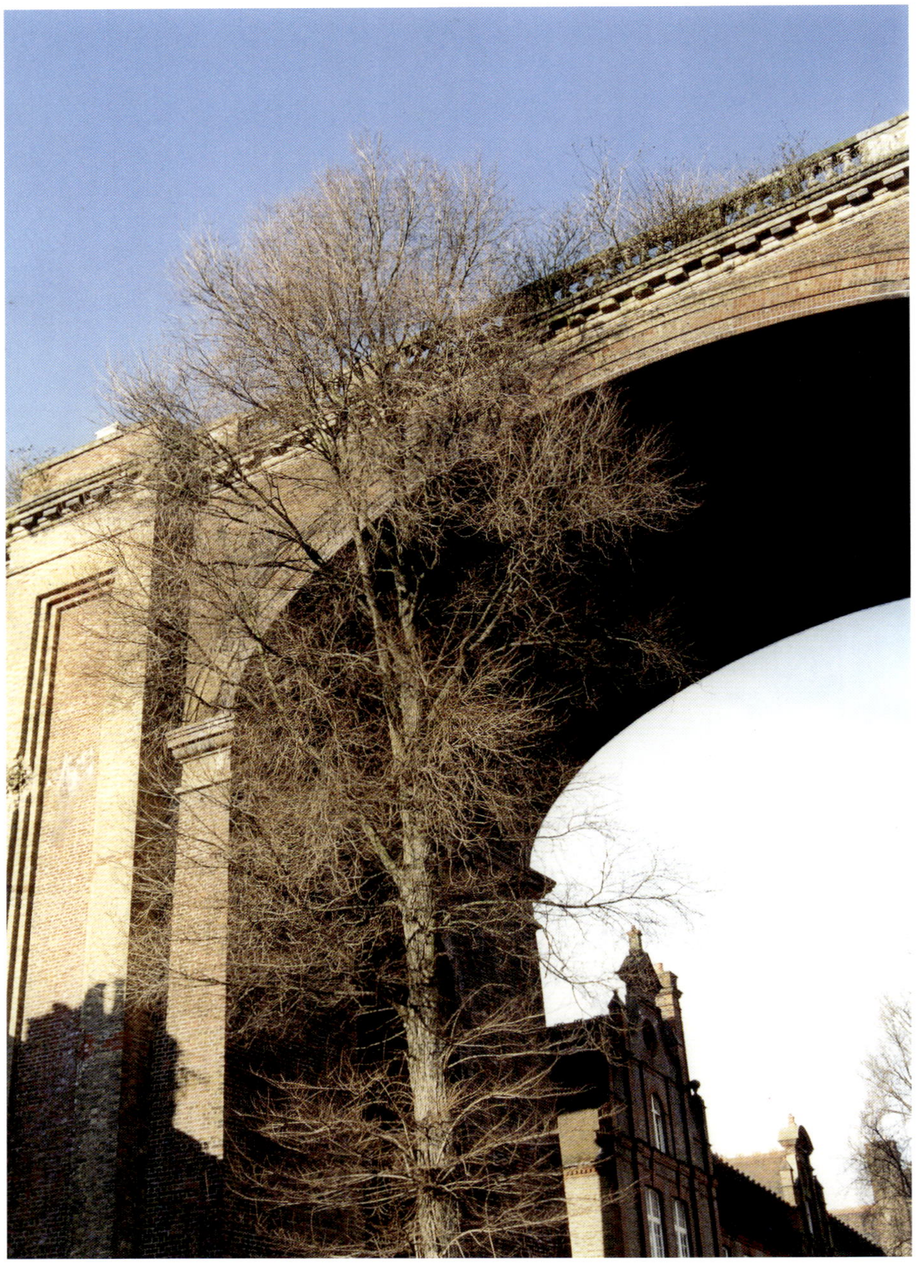

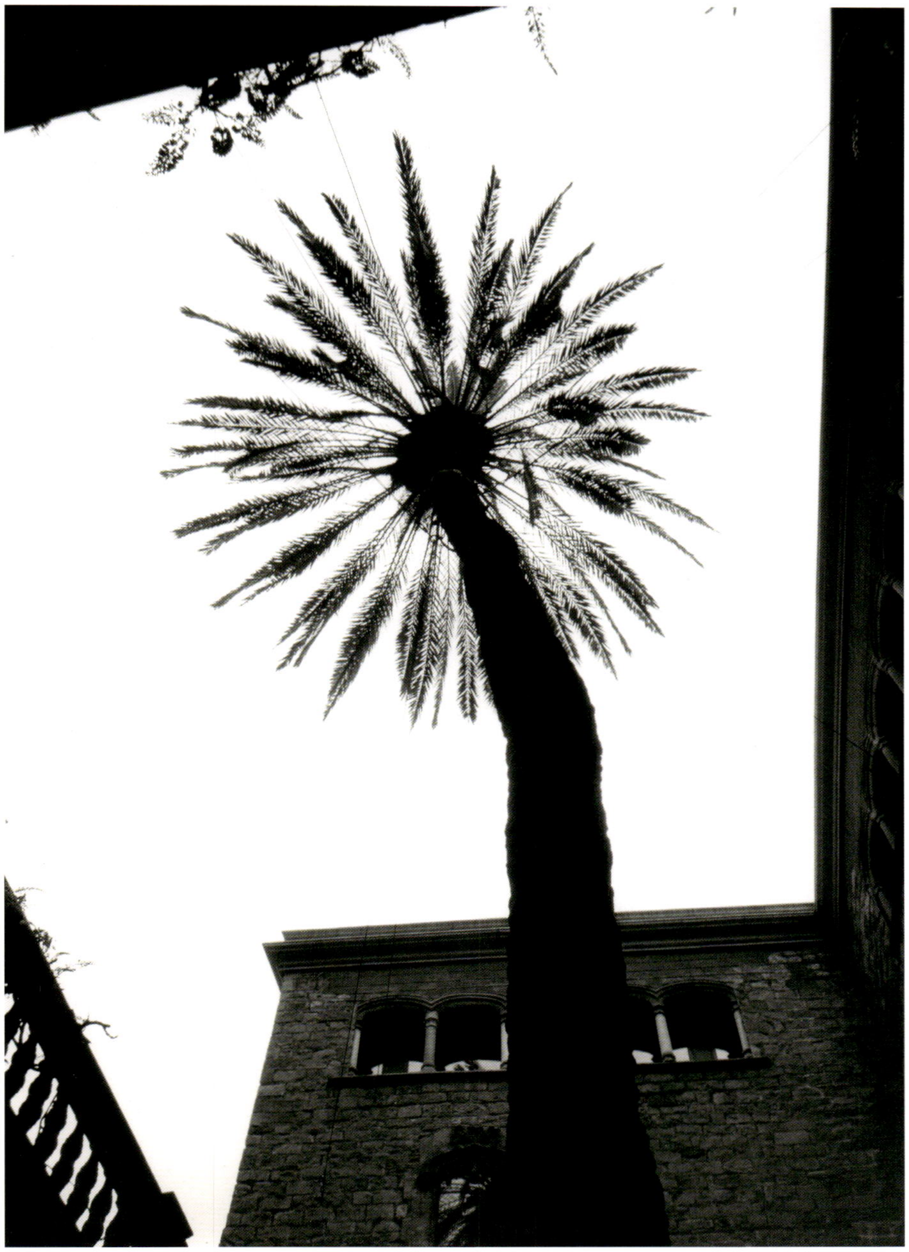

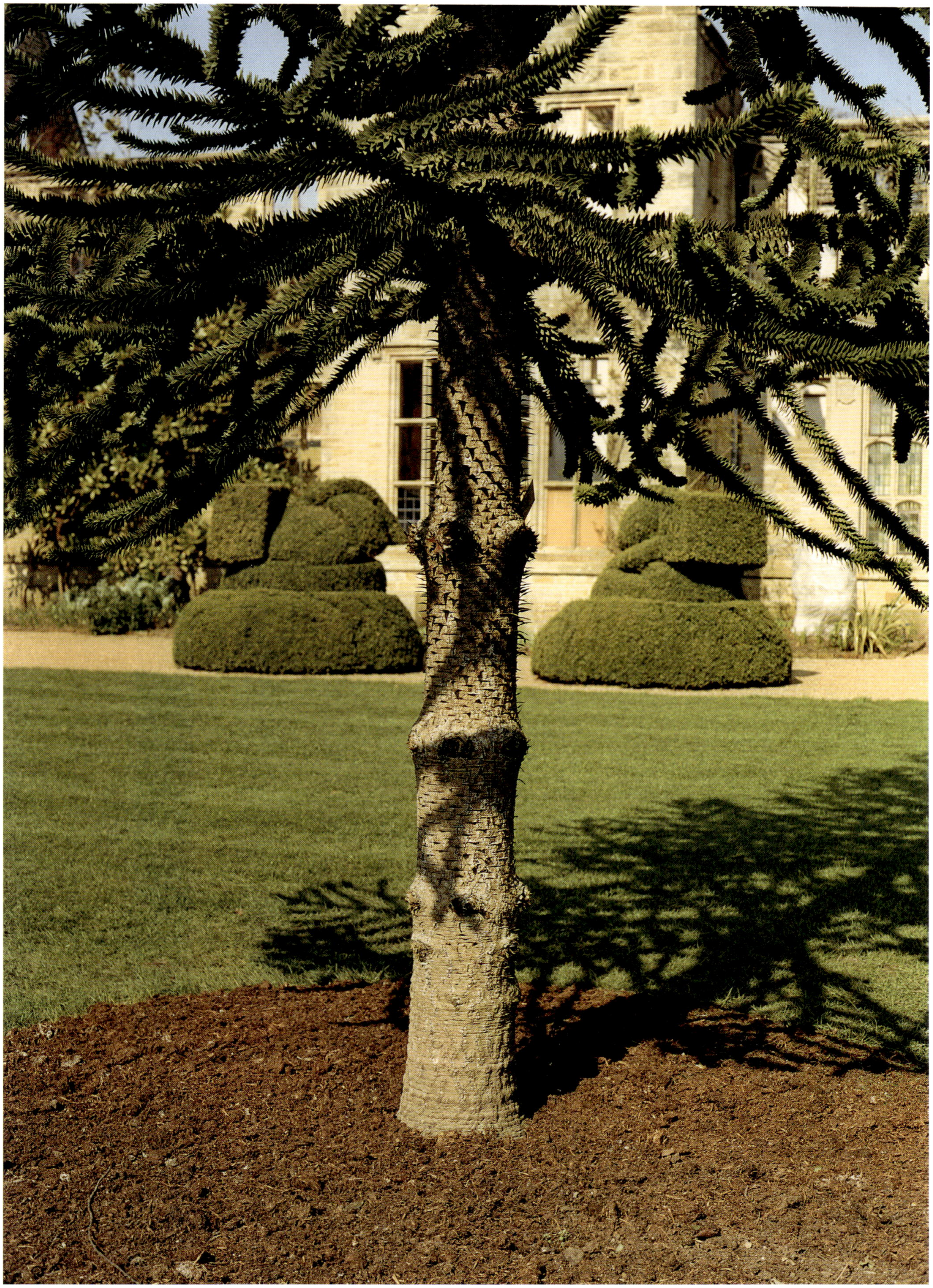

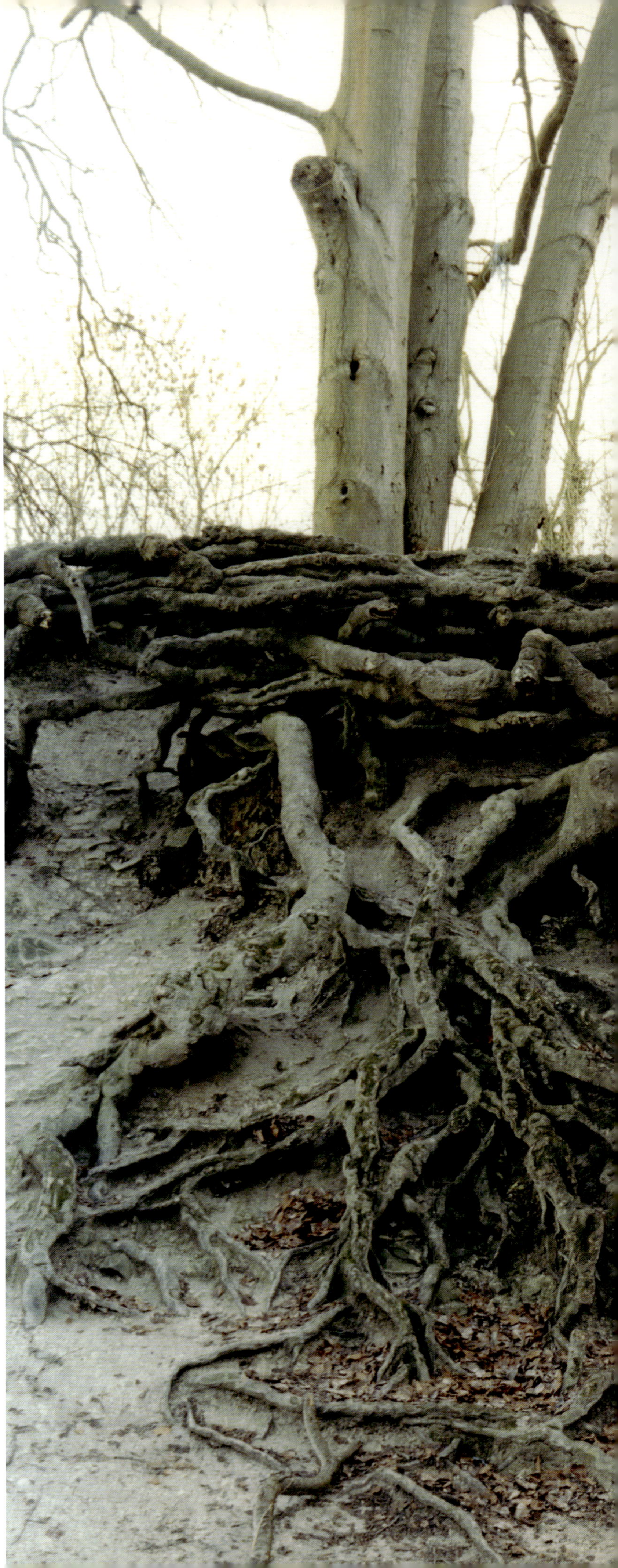

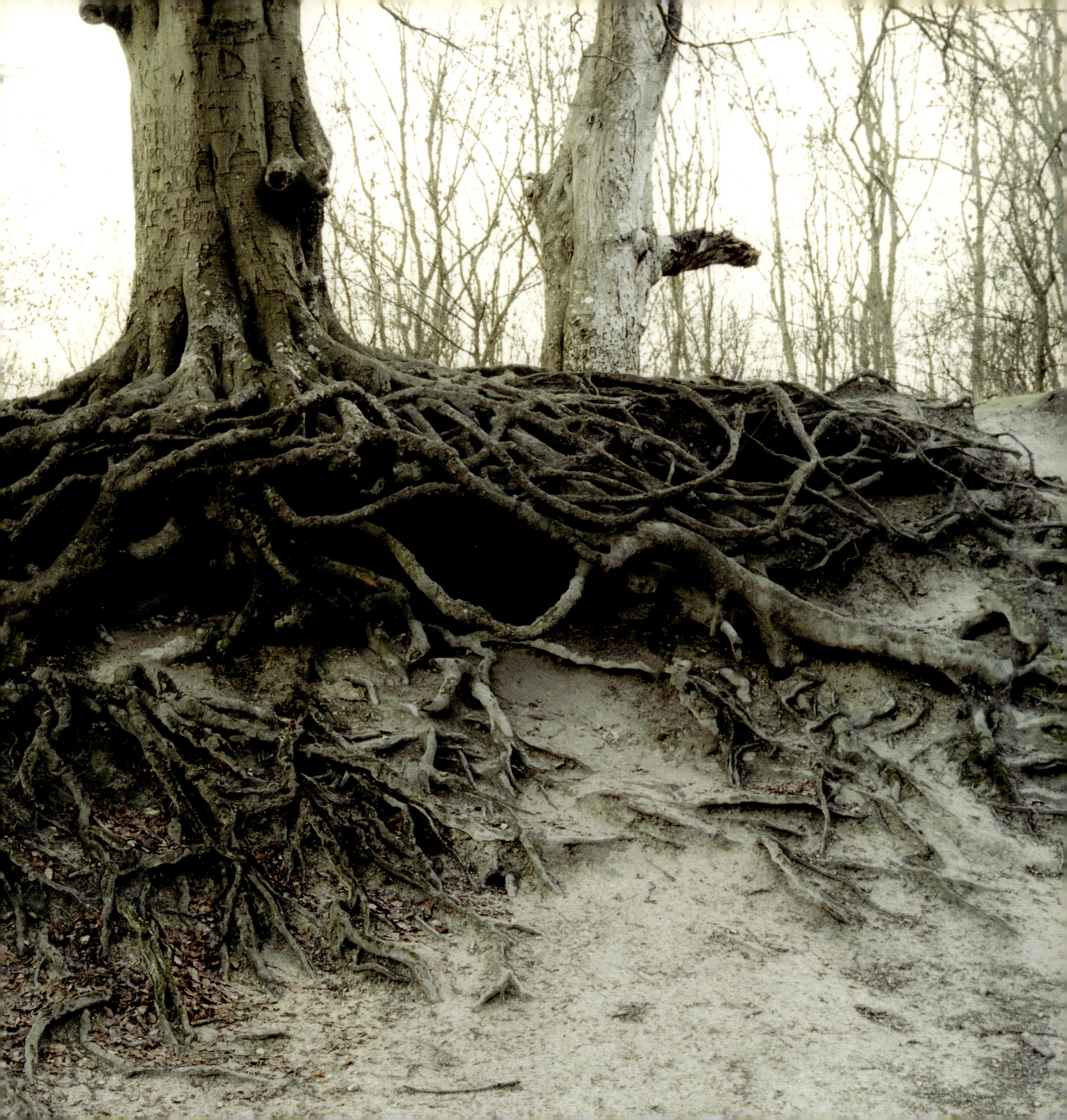

They are beautiful in their peace, they are wise in their silence.
They will stand after we are dust. They teach us, and we tend them.

Galeain Ip Altiem Mac Dunelmore, ca.1848

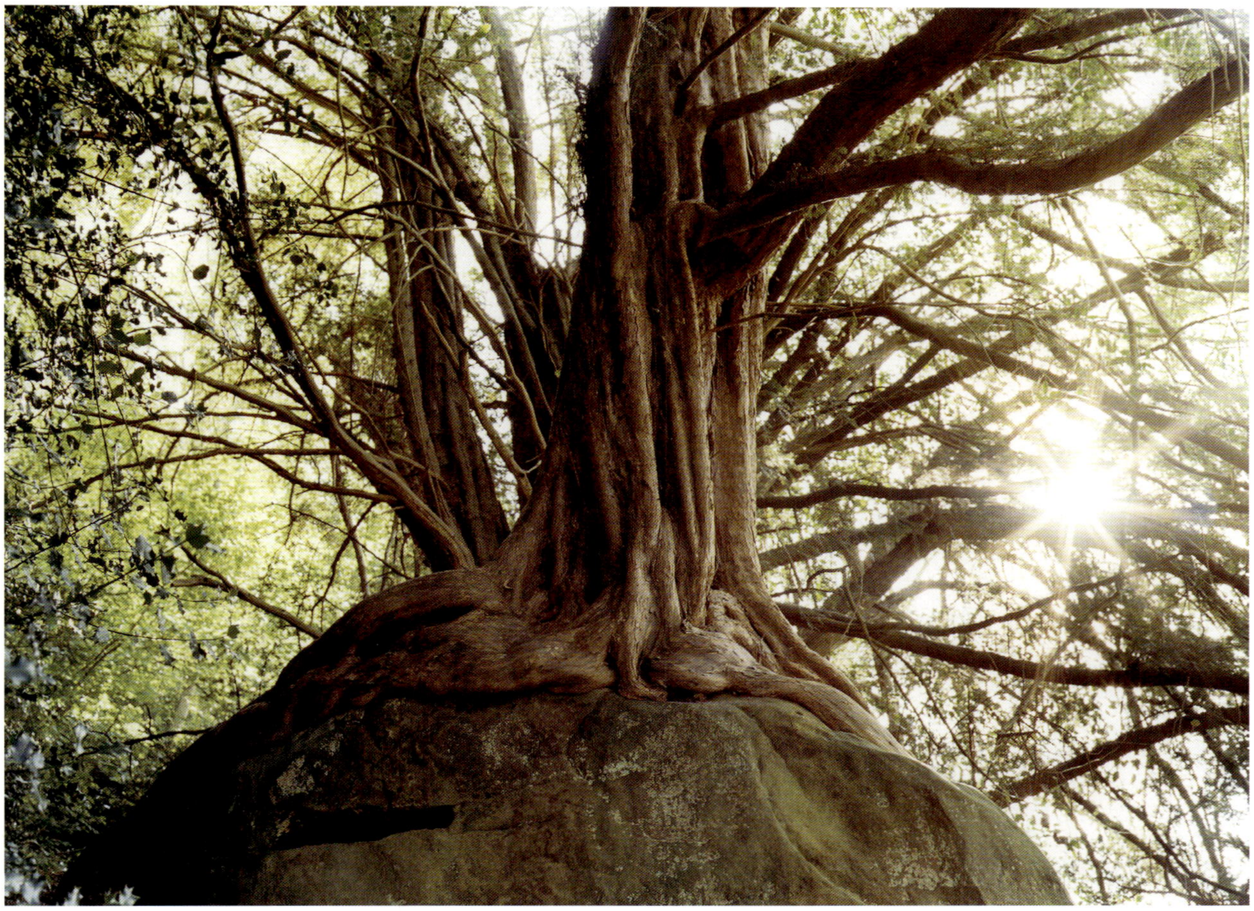

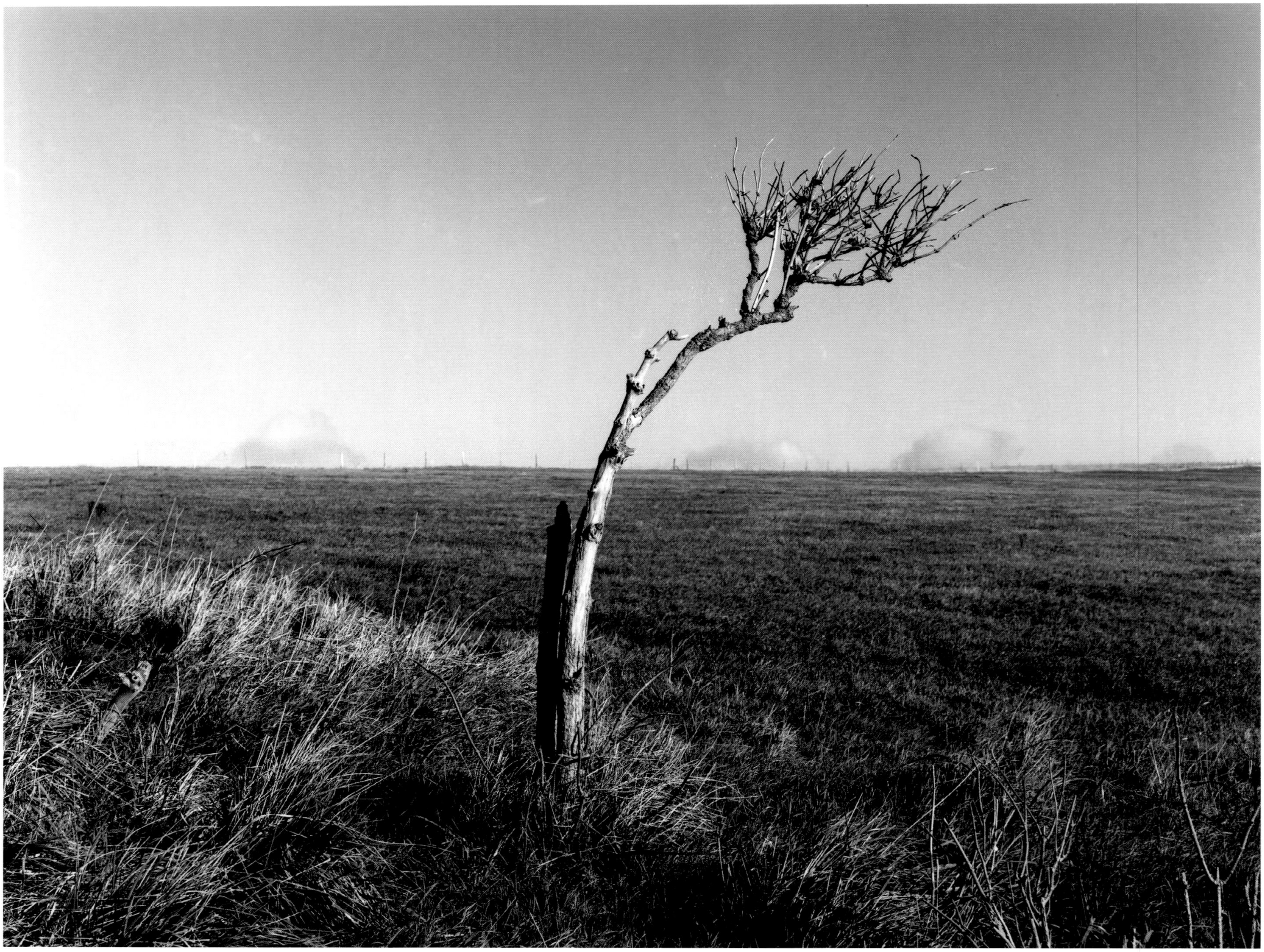

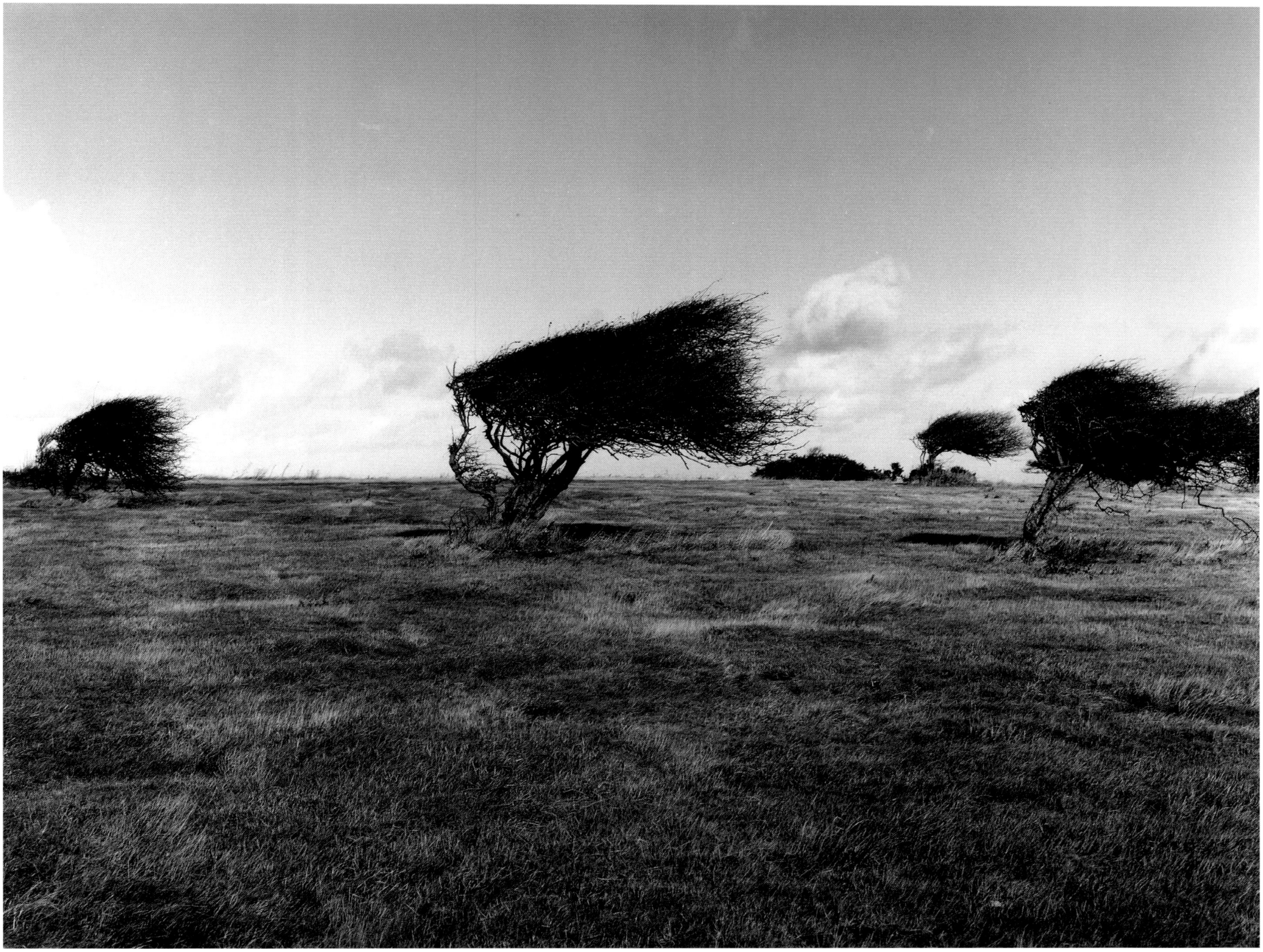

A tree does not move unless there is wind.

Afghan Proverb

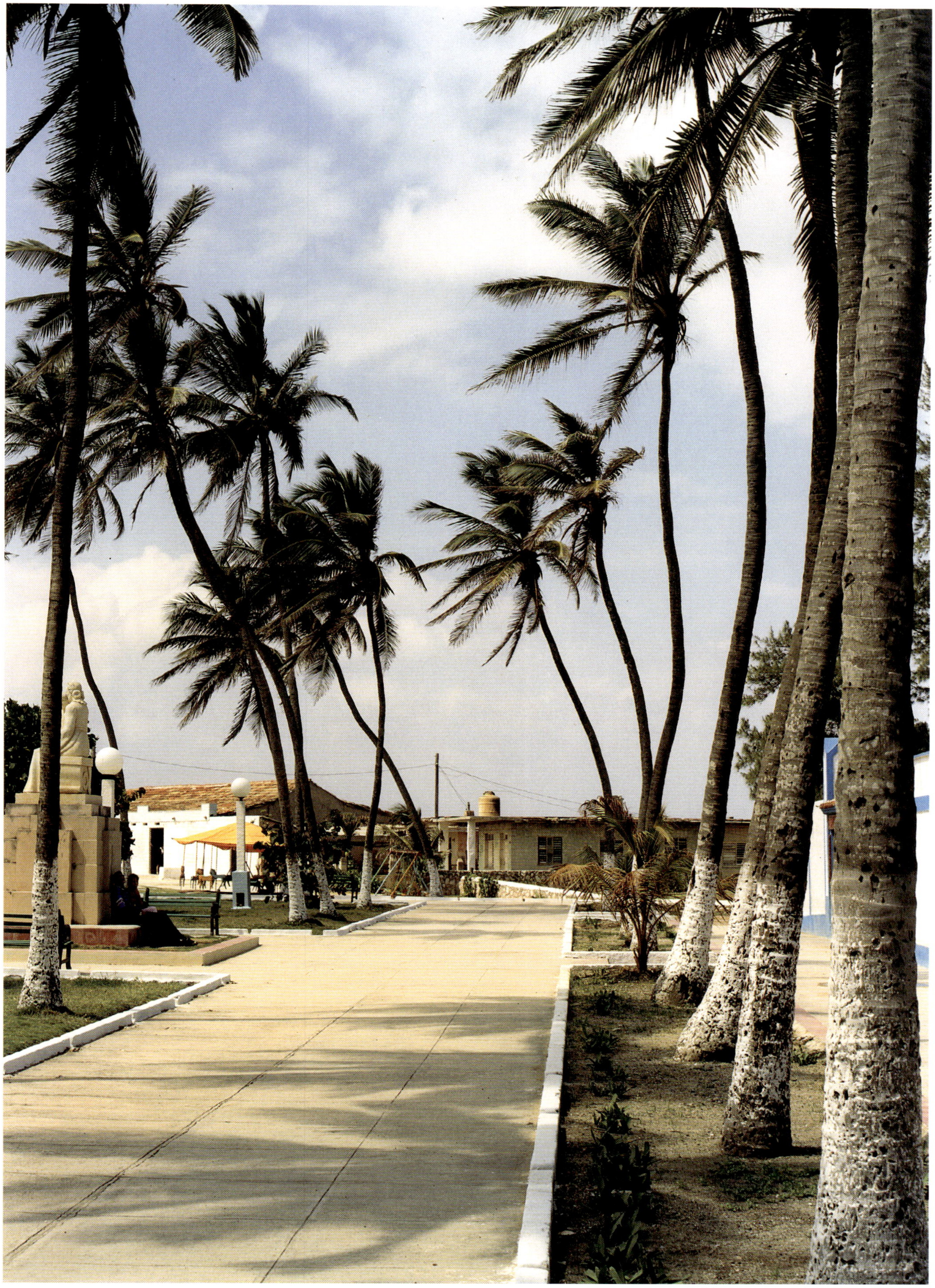

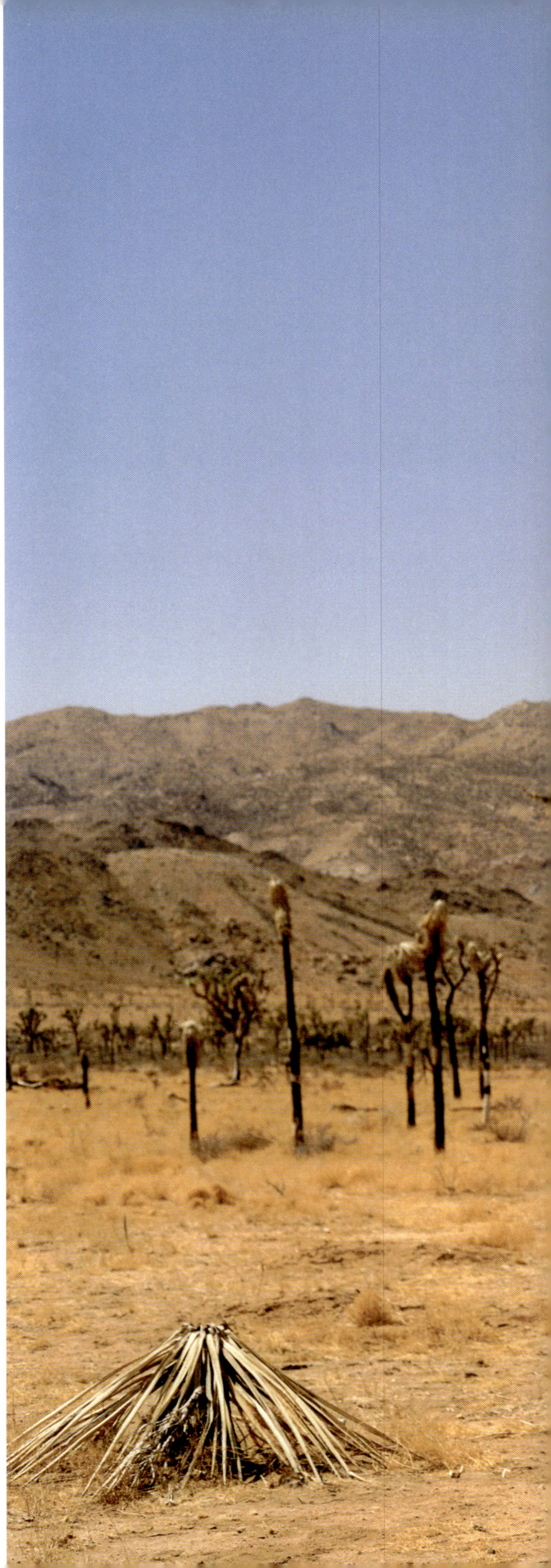

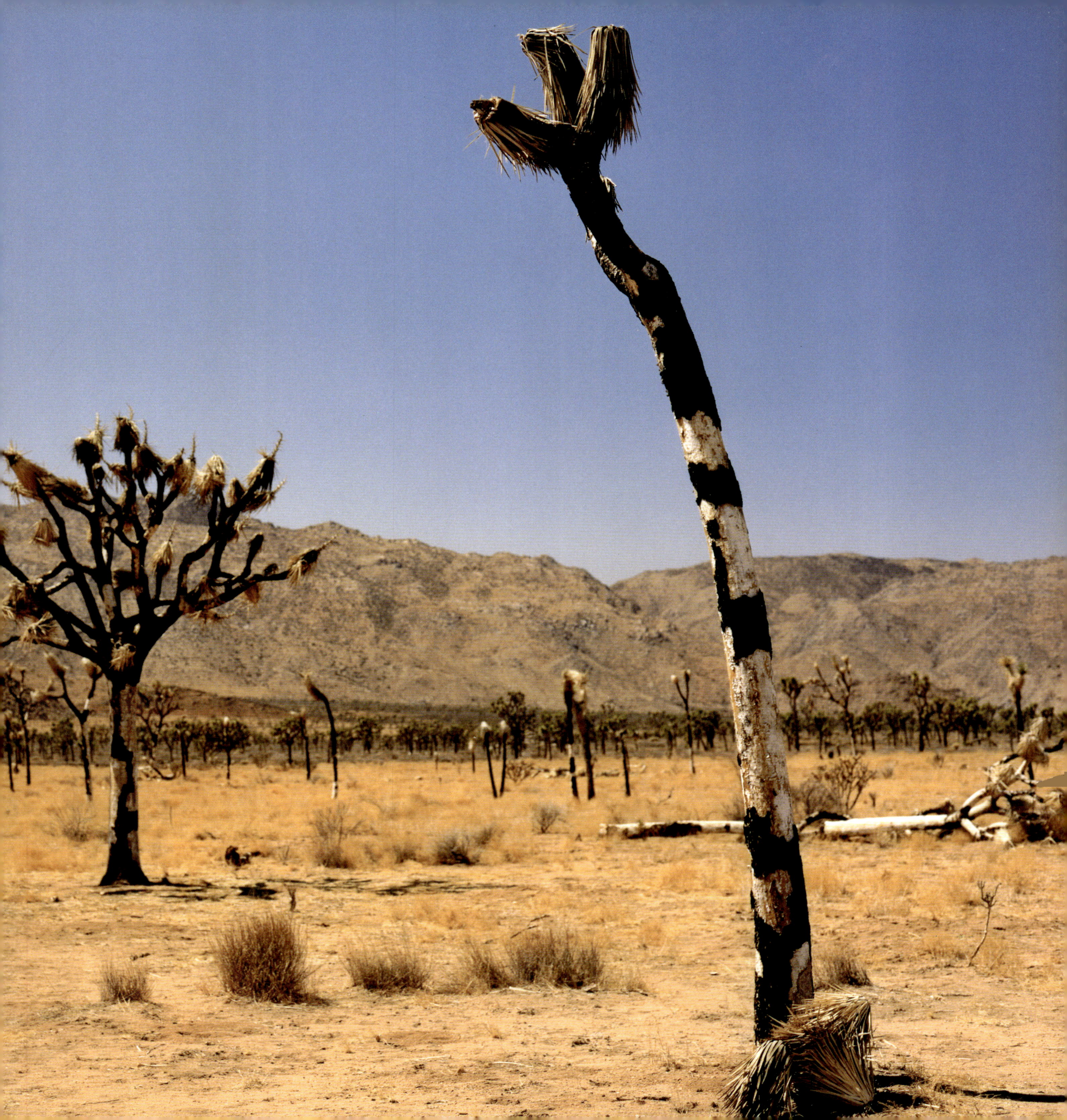

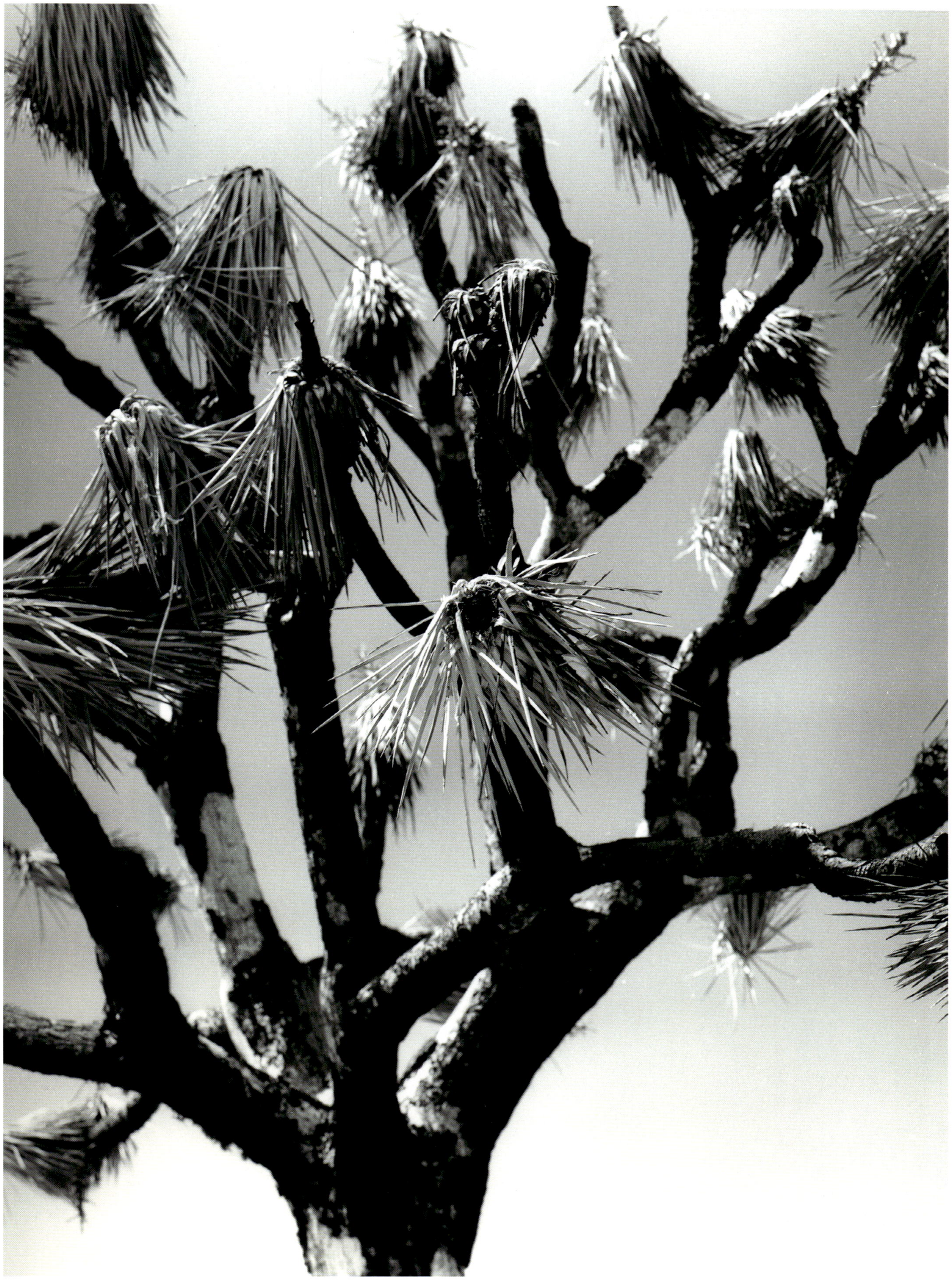

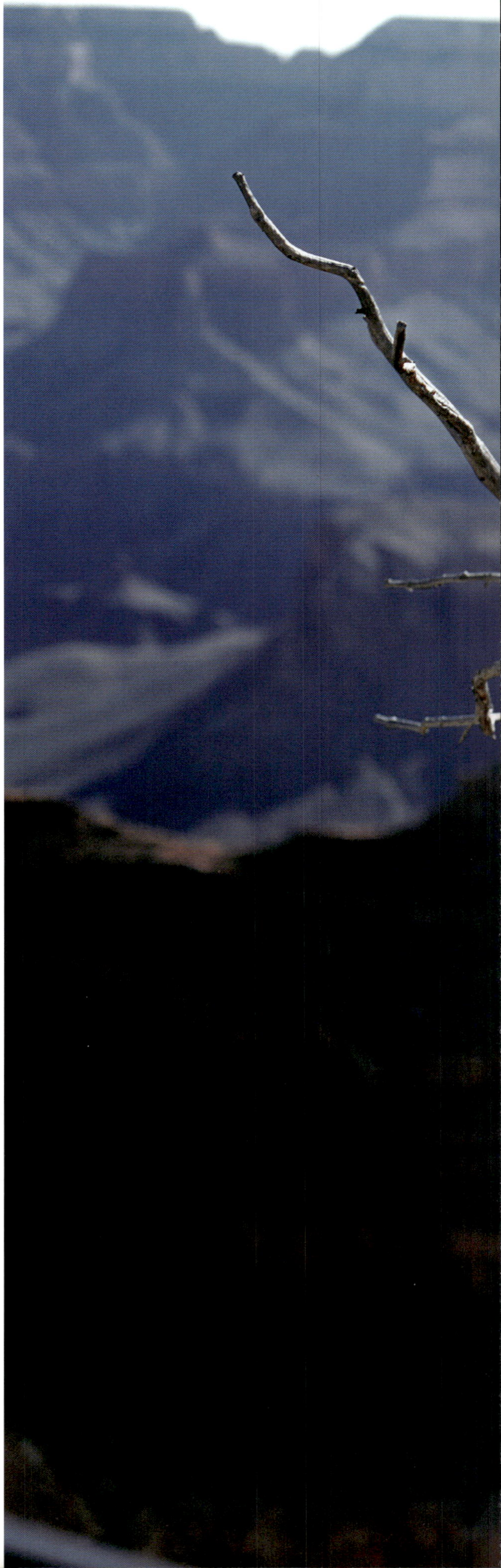

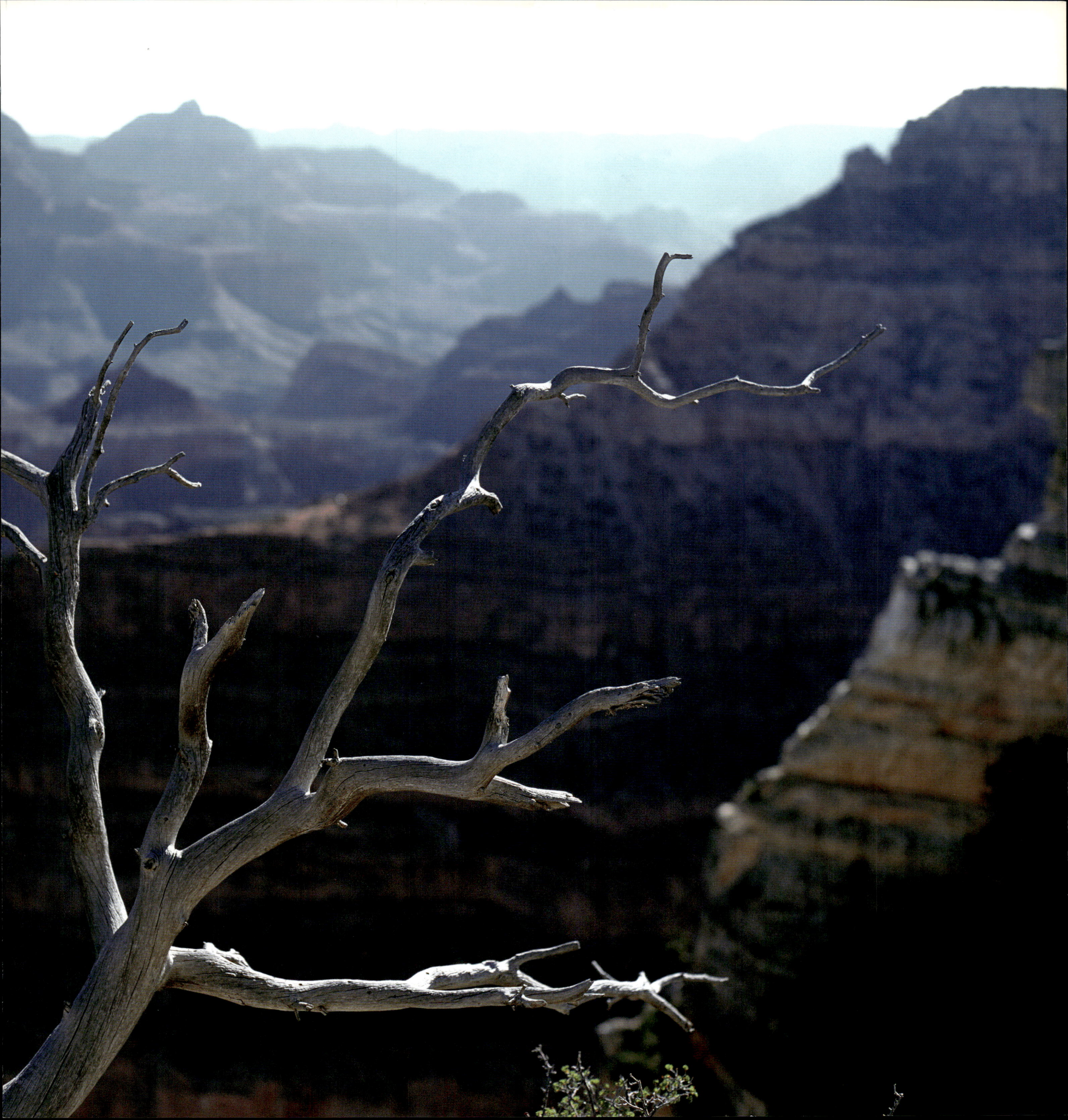

RECLAIM

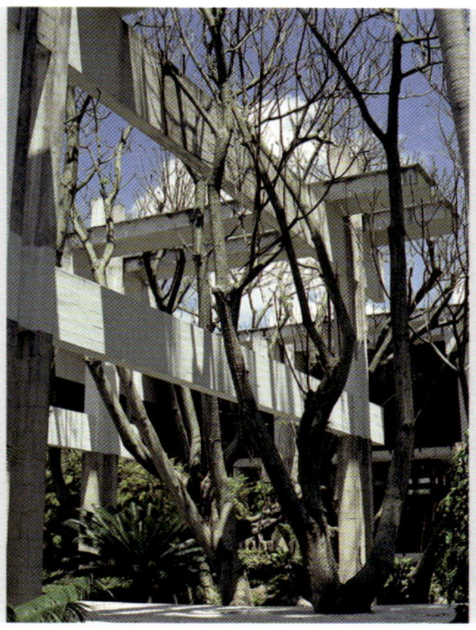

There's a tree that grows in Brooklyn.
Some people call it the tree of Heaven.
No matter where its seed falls, it makes a tree
which struggles to reach the sky.
It grows in boarded up plots
and out of neglected rubbish heaps.
It grows out of cellar gratings.
It is the only tree that grows out of cement.
It grows lushly... survives without sun, water and
seemingly without earth.
It would be considered beautiful except
that there are to many of it.

Betty Smith, 1896- 1972

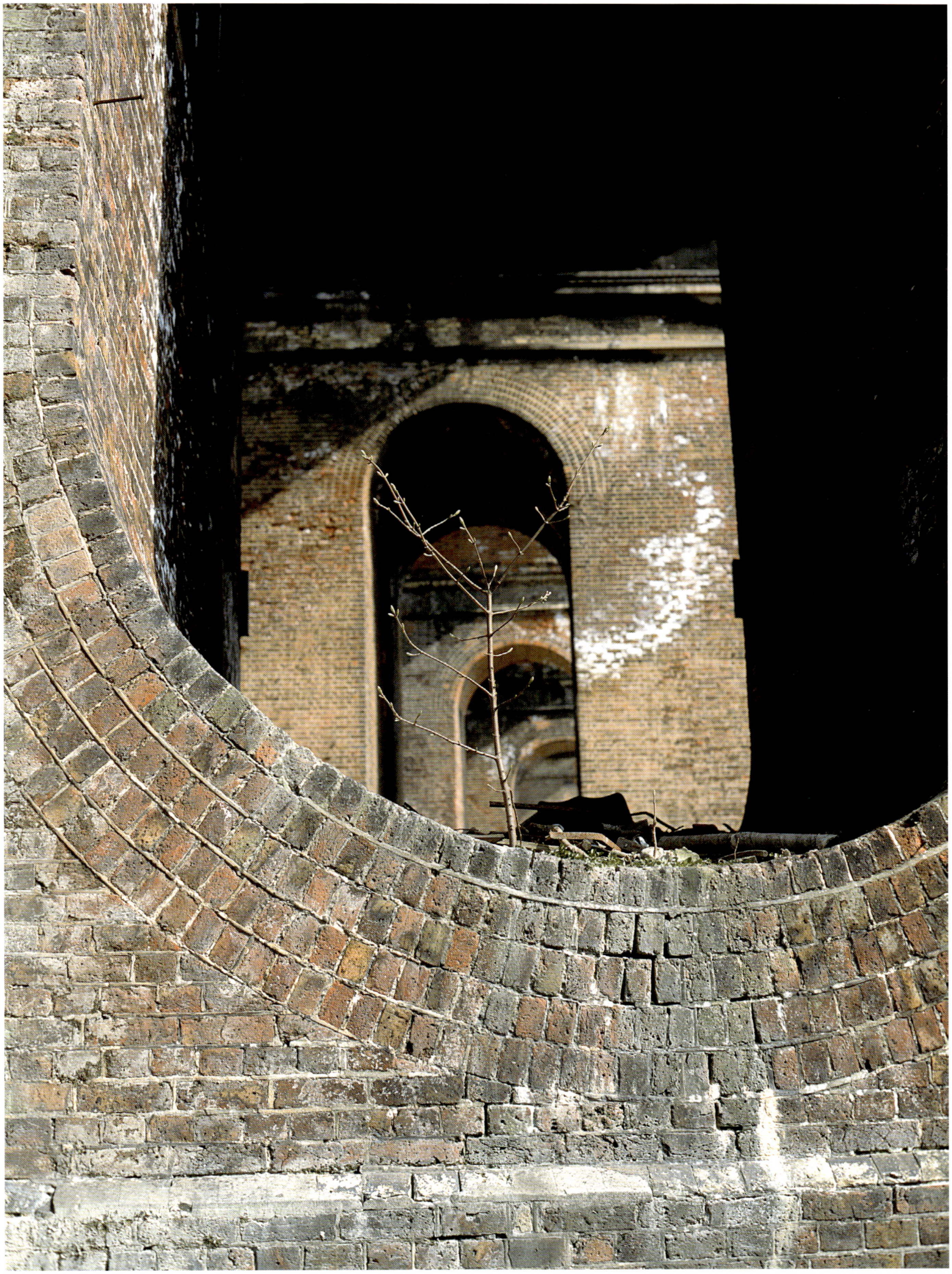

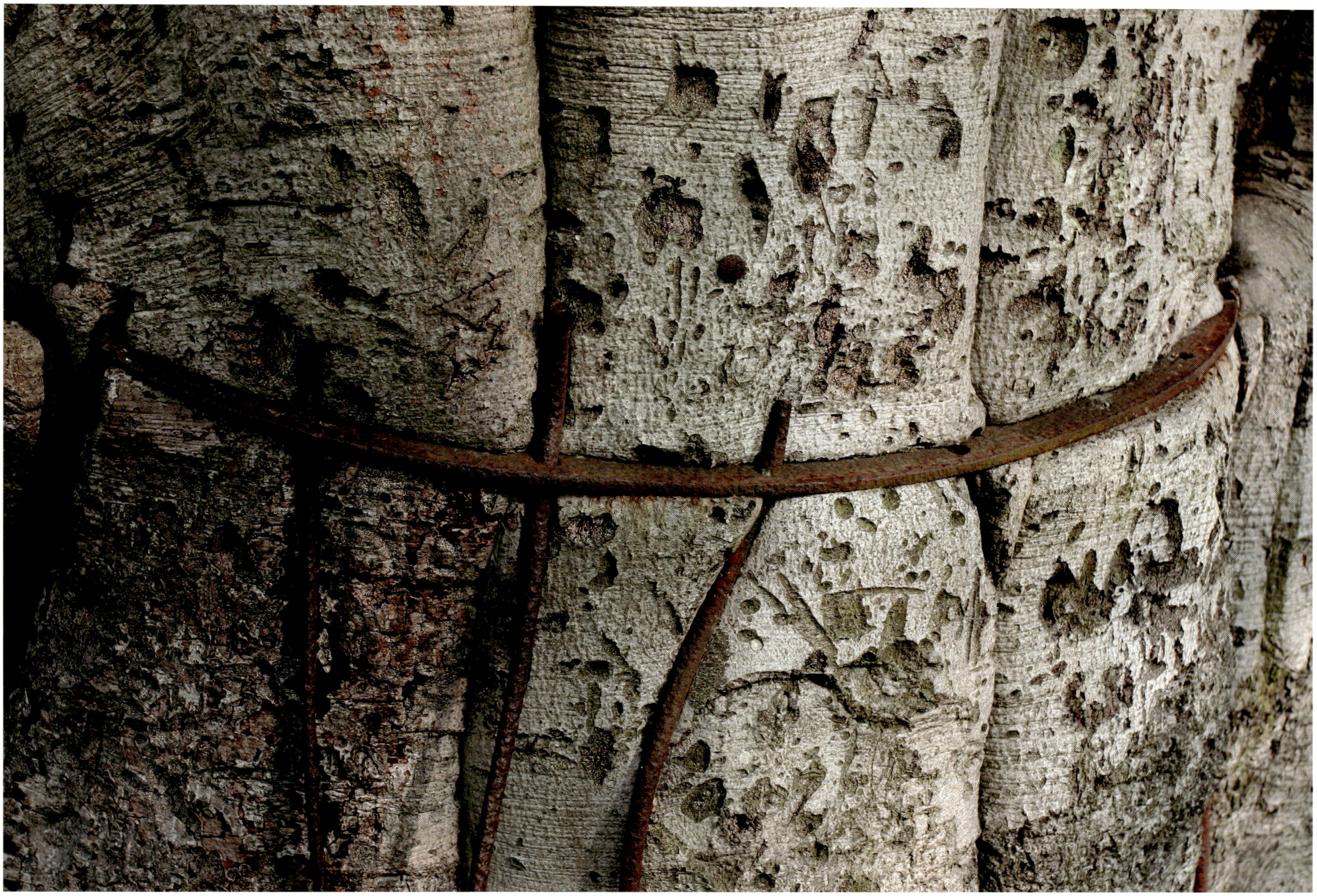

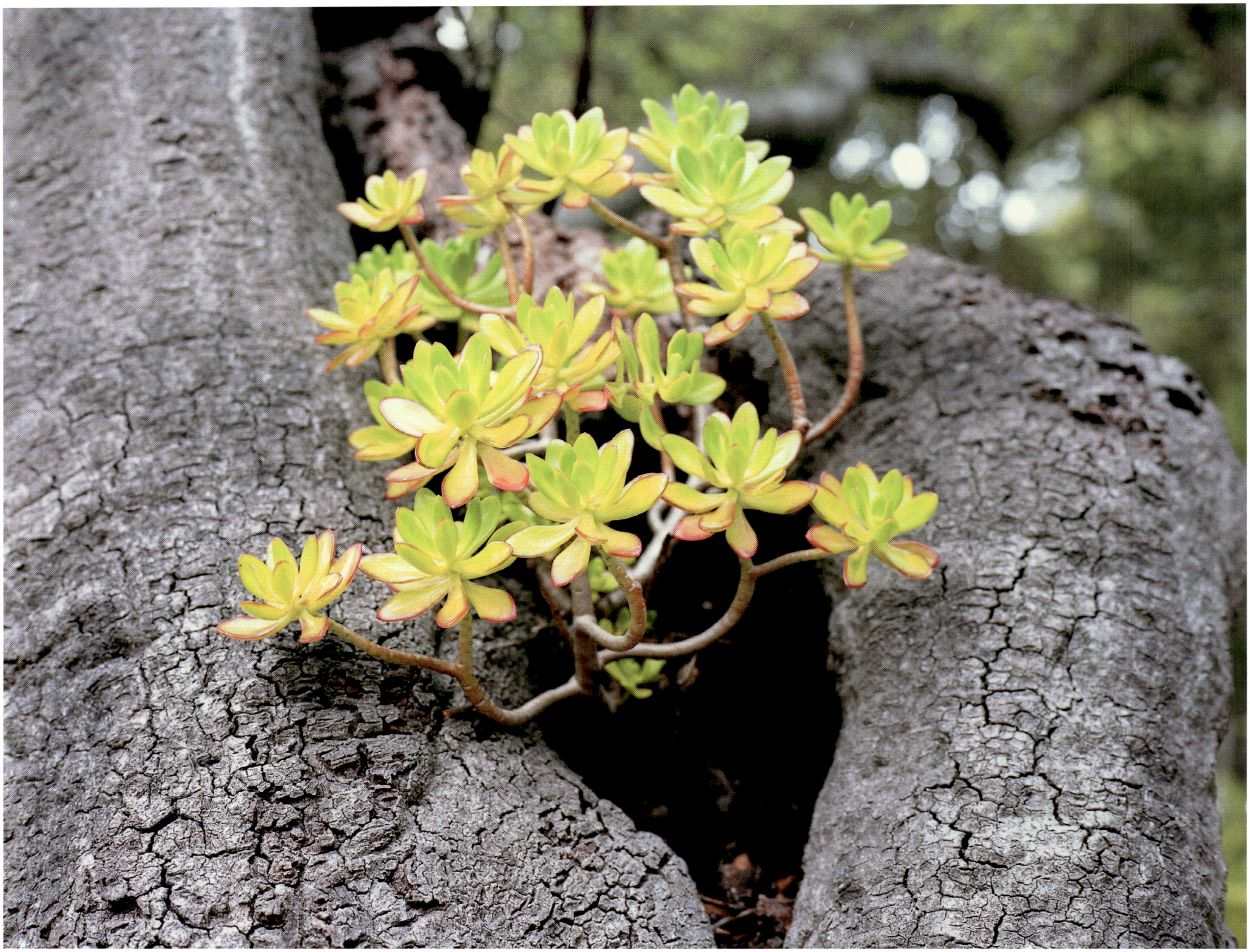

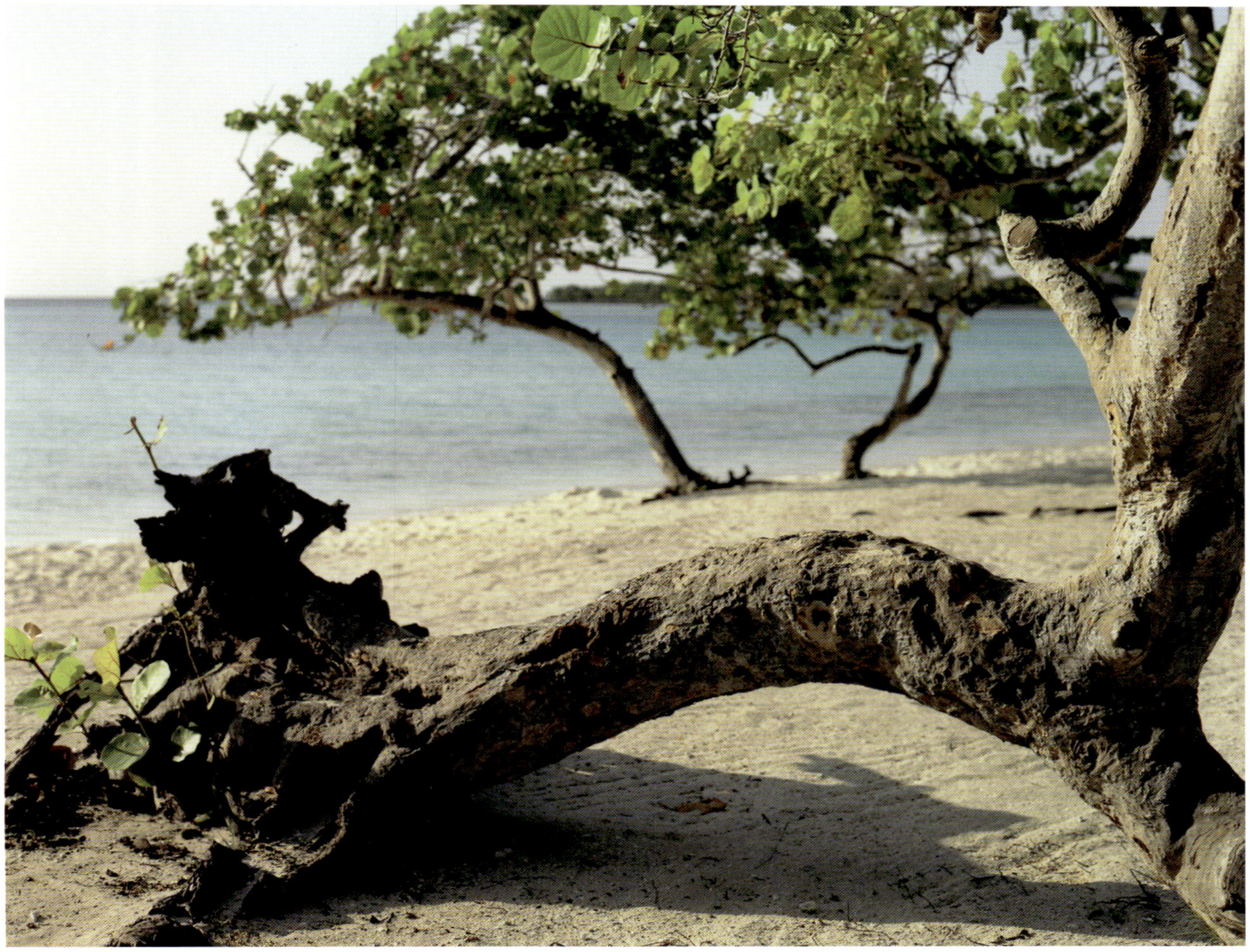

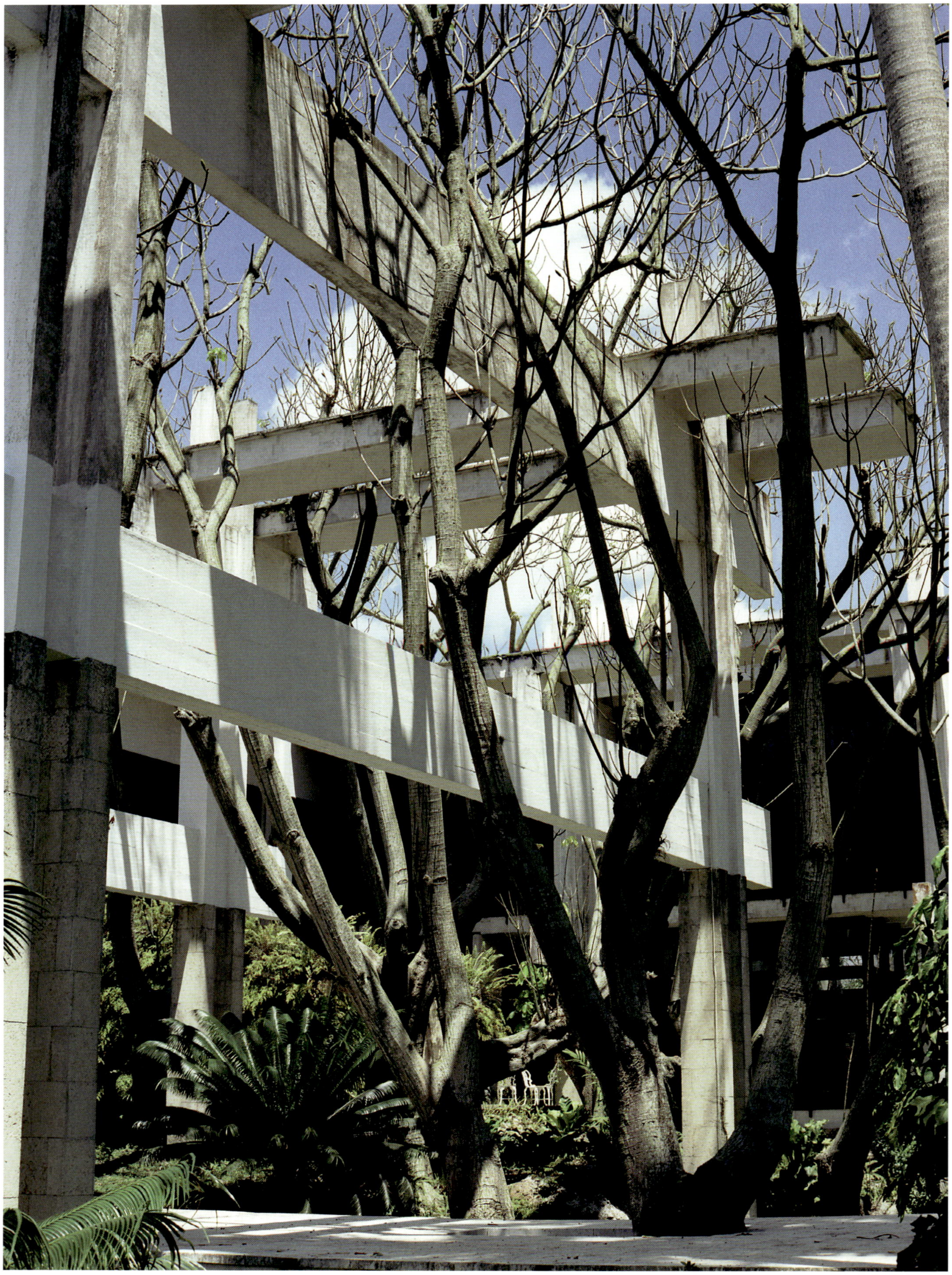

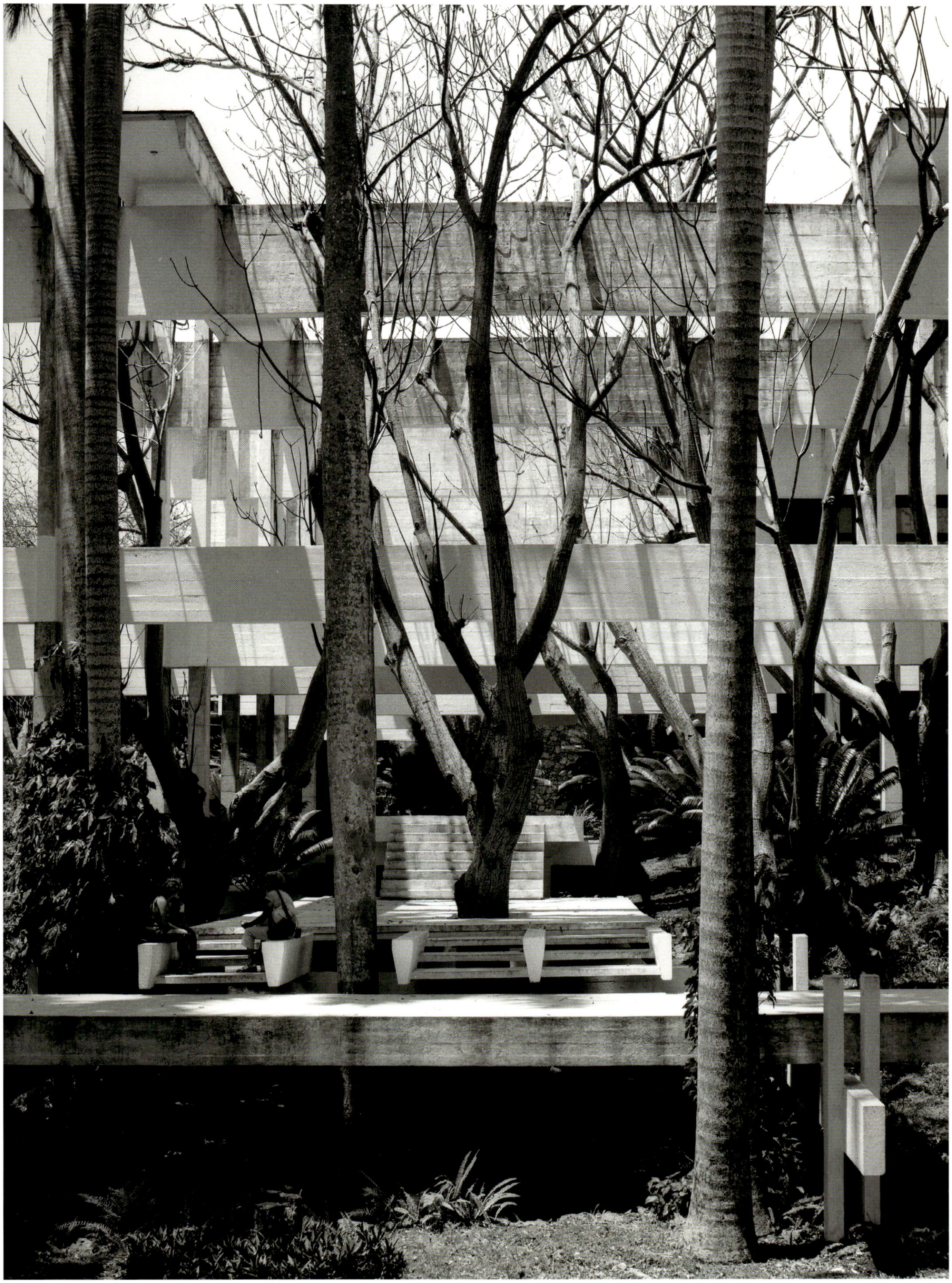

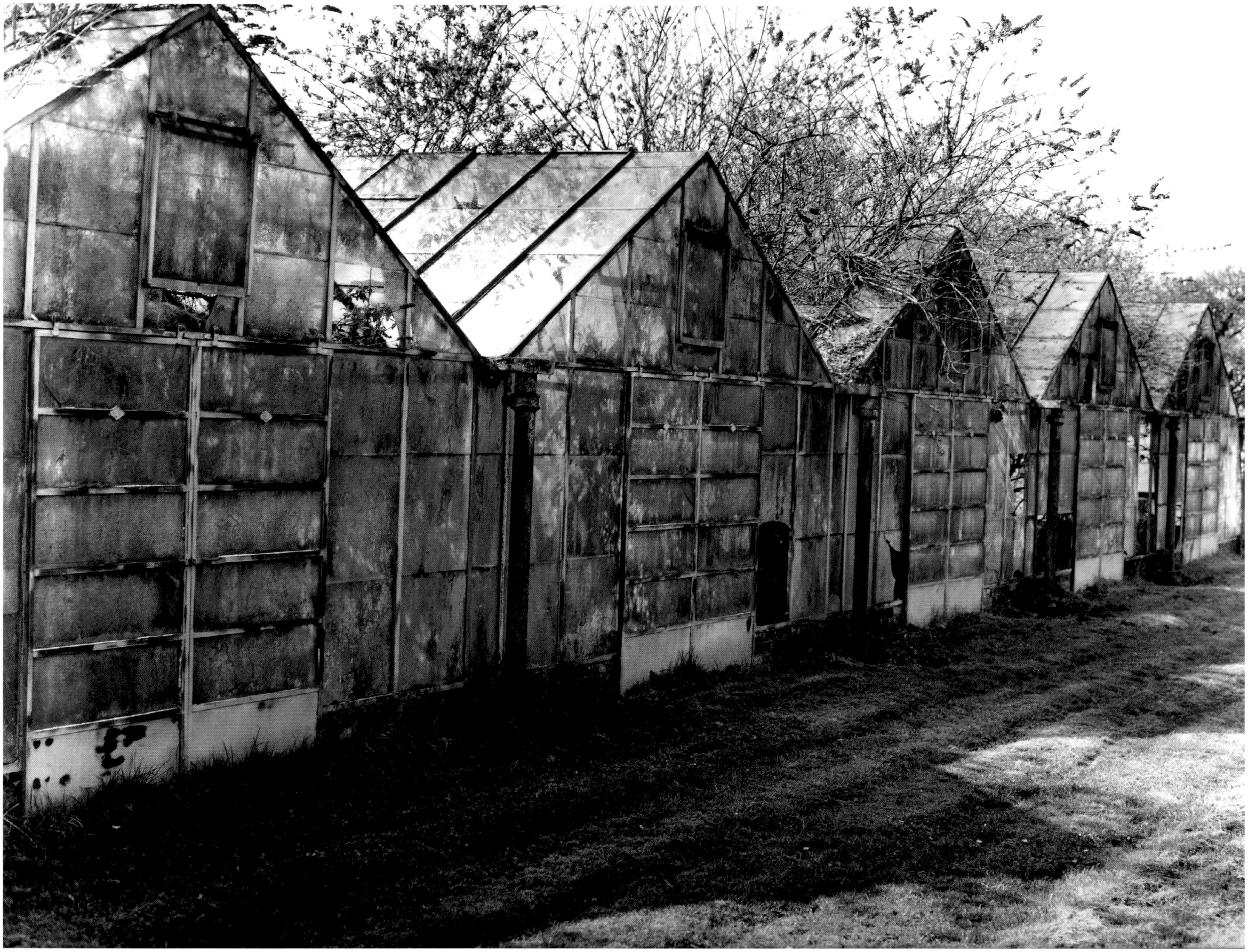

The wonder is that we can see these trees and not wonder more.

Ralph Waldo Emerson, 1803-1882

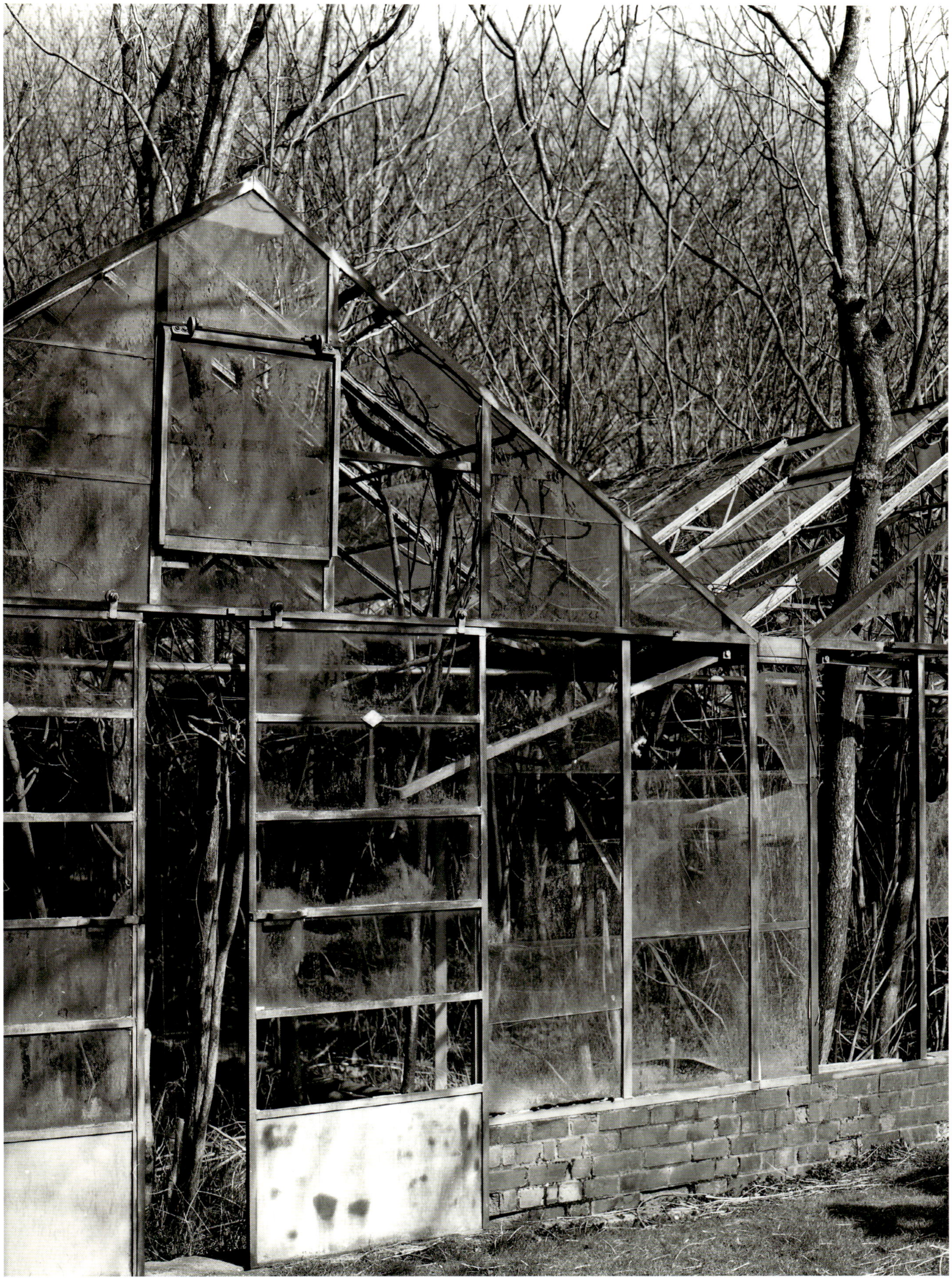

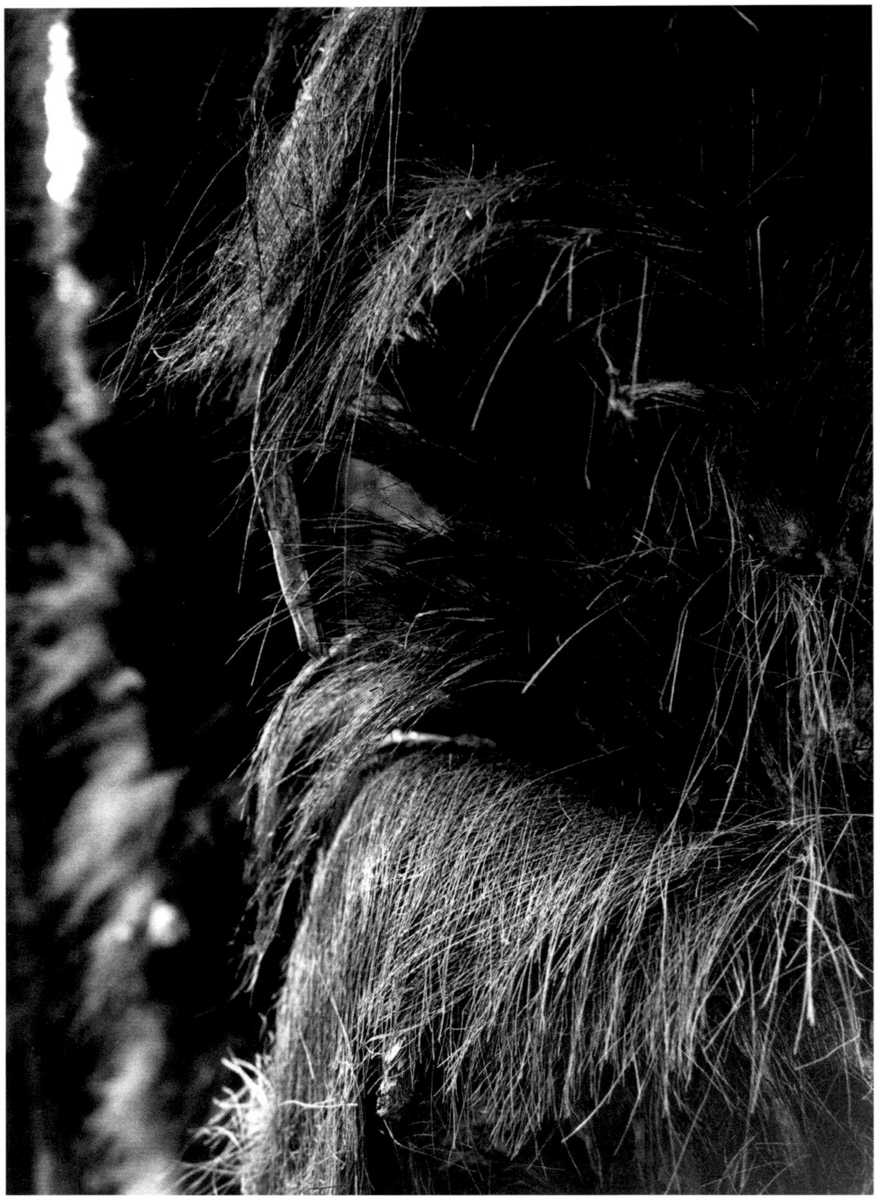

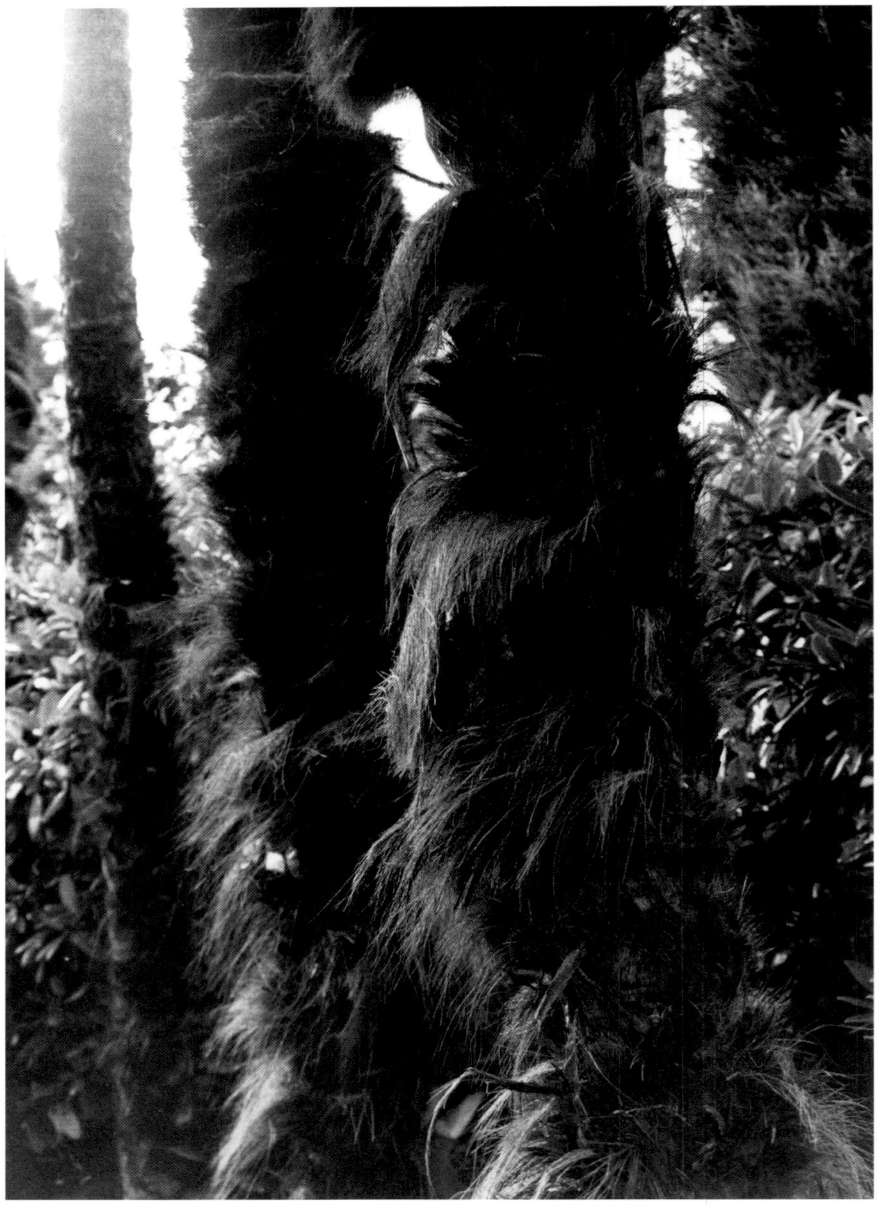

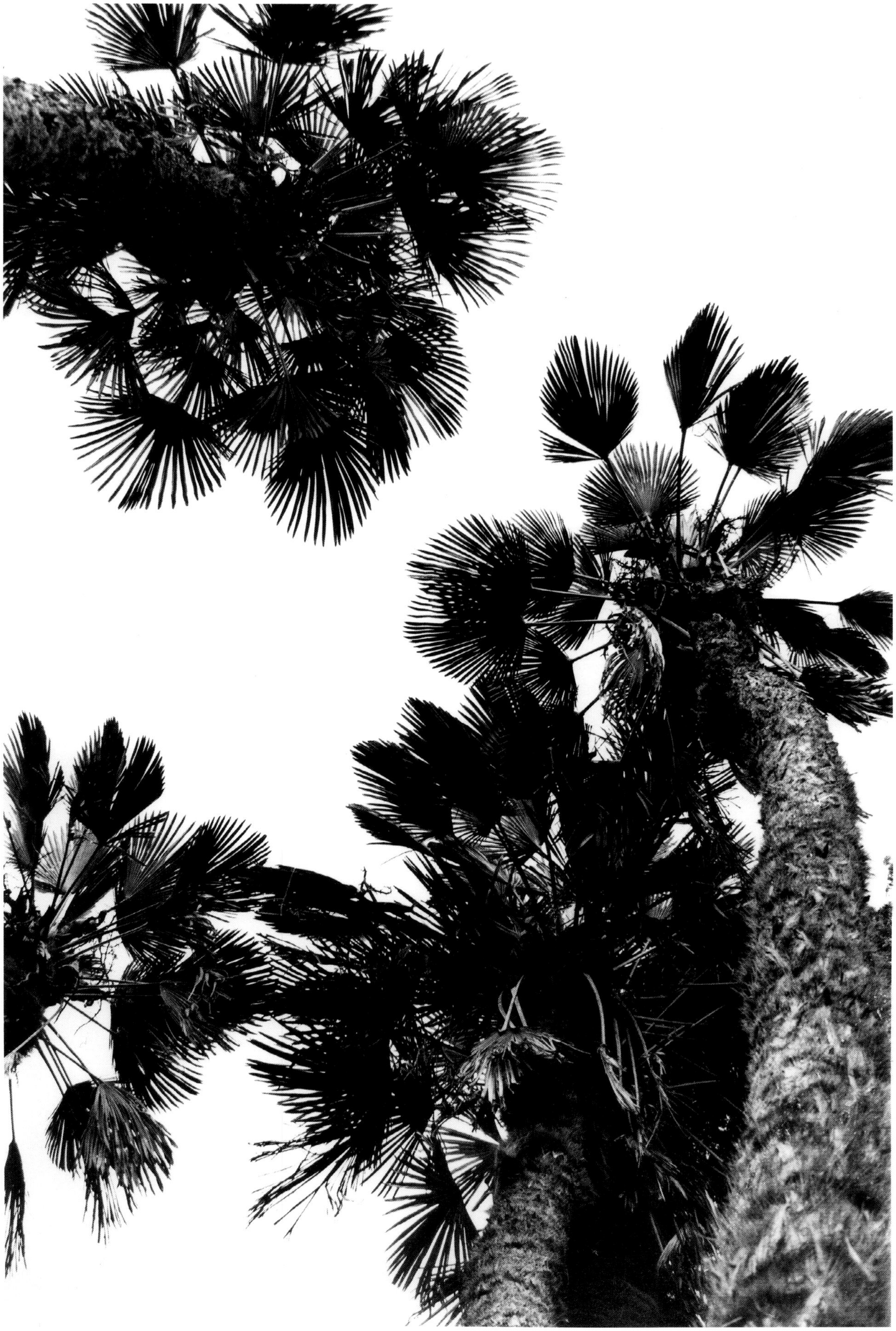

PARTICIPATE

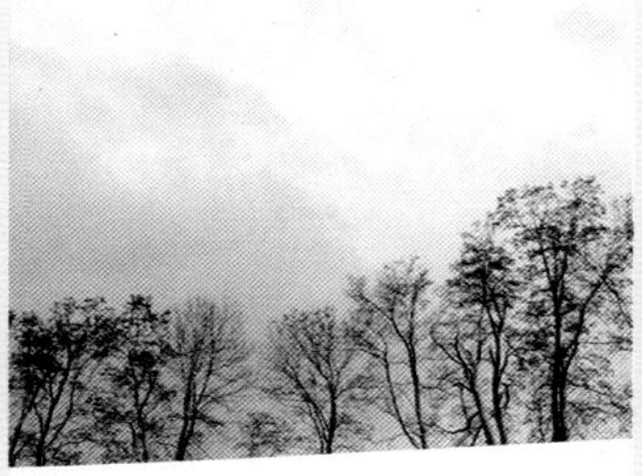

All it has experienced, tasted, suffered;
the course of years , generations of animals,
oppression, recovery, friendship of sun and wind
will pour forth each day in the song
of its rustling foliage, in the friendly
gesture of its gently swaying crown,
in the delicate sweet scent of resinous
sap moistening the sleep-glued buds,
and the eternal game of lights and
shadows it plays with itself, content.

Herman Hesse, 1877-1962

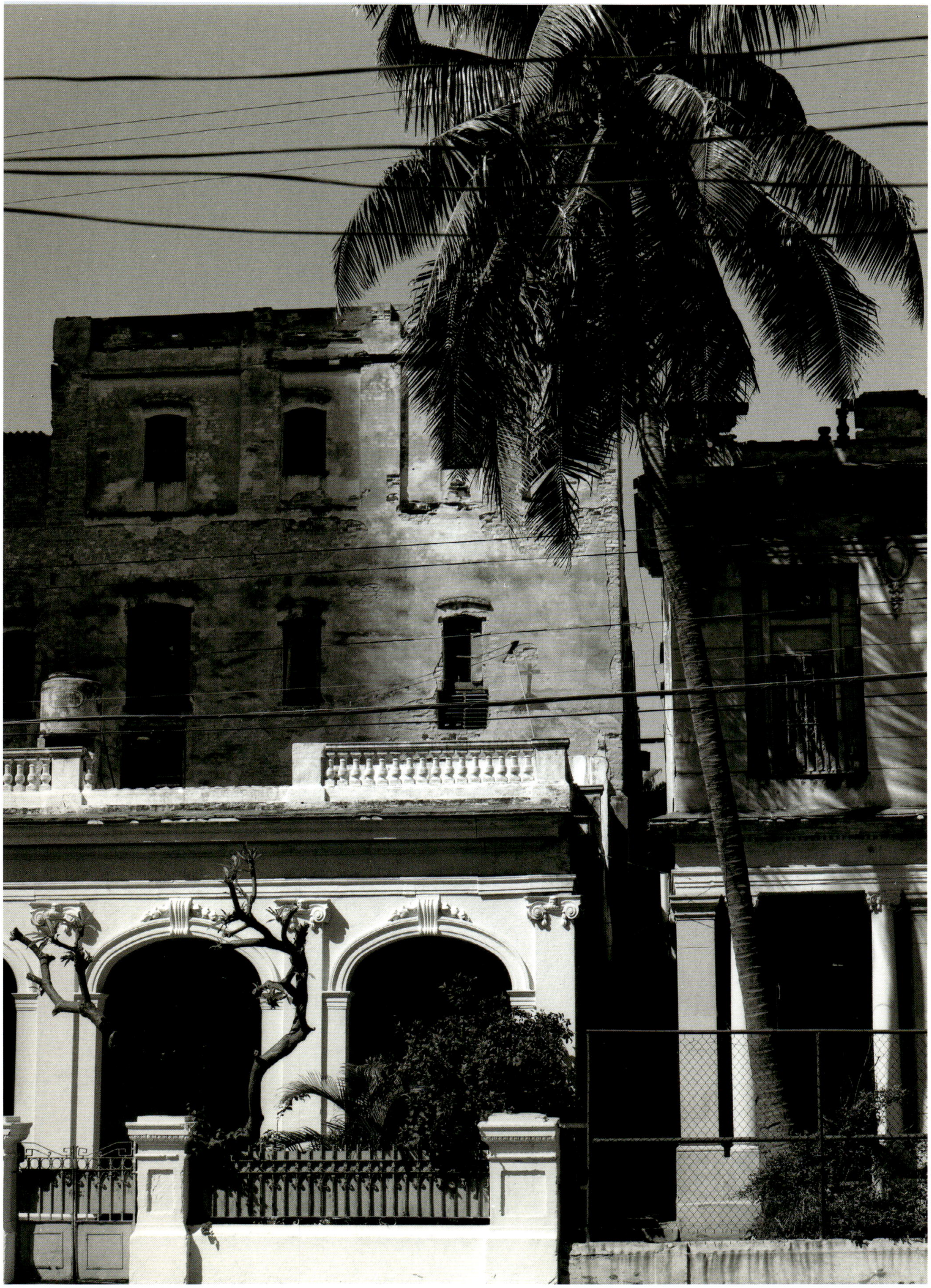

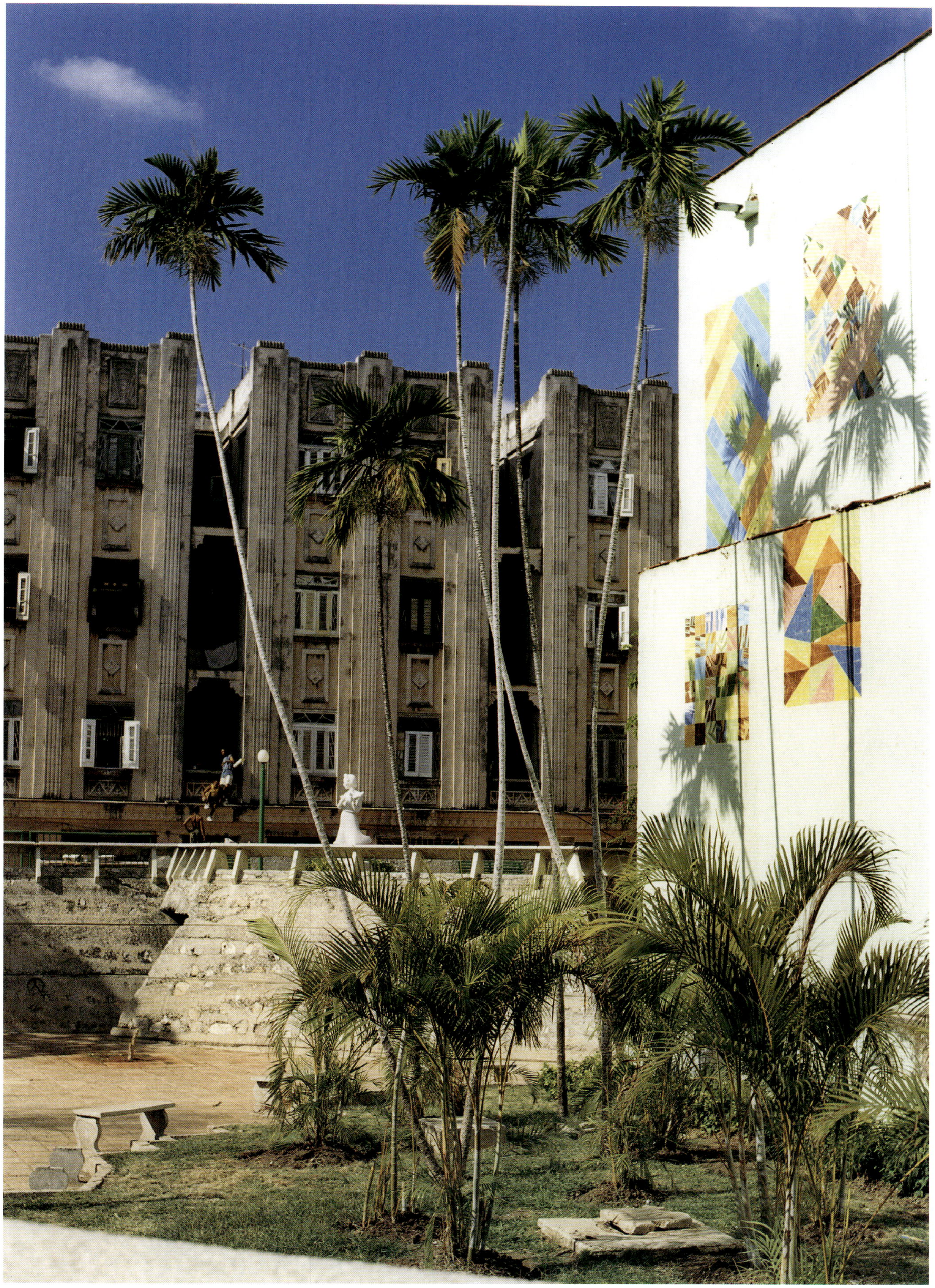

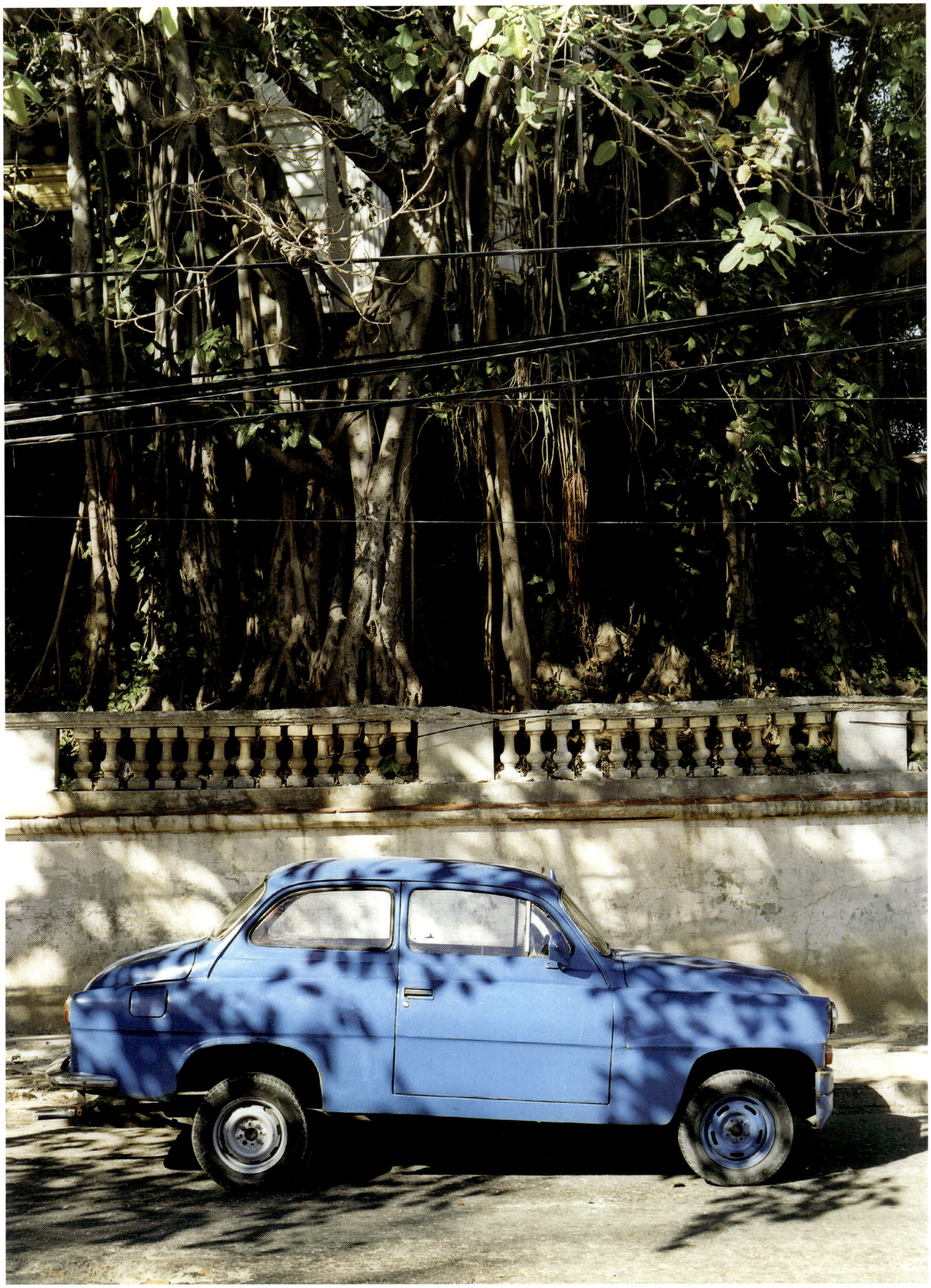

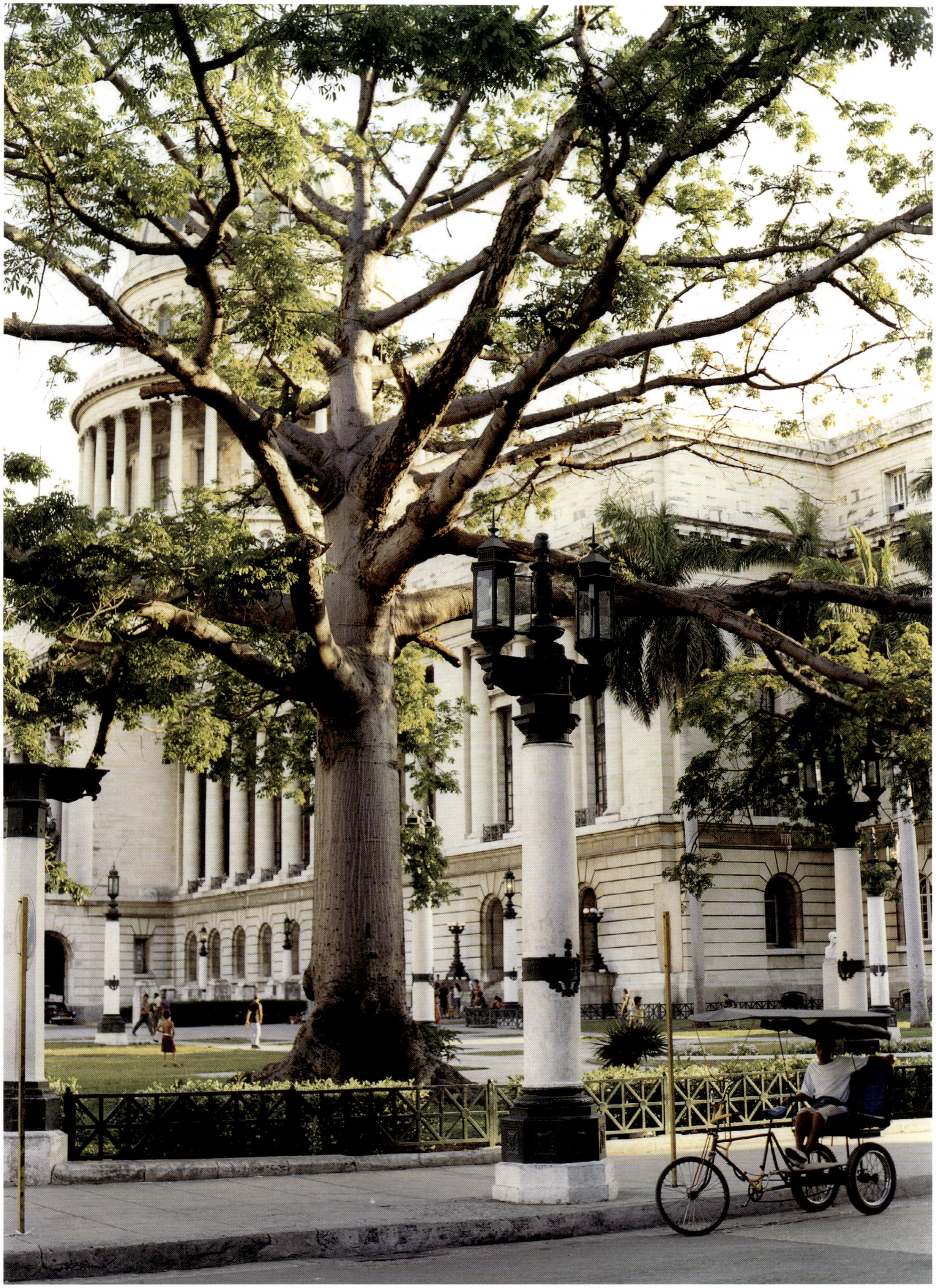

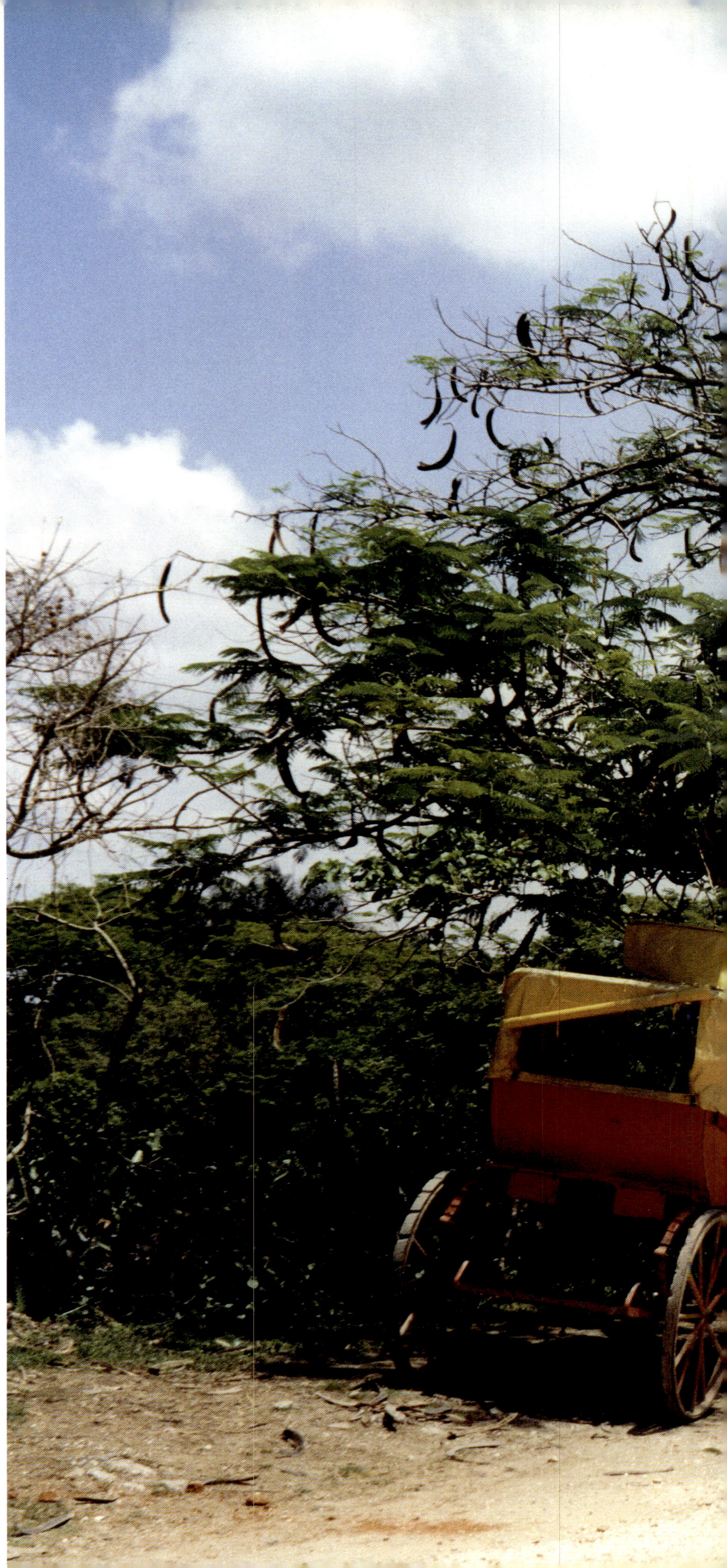

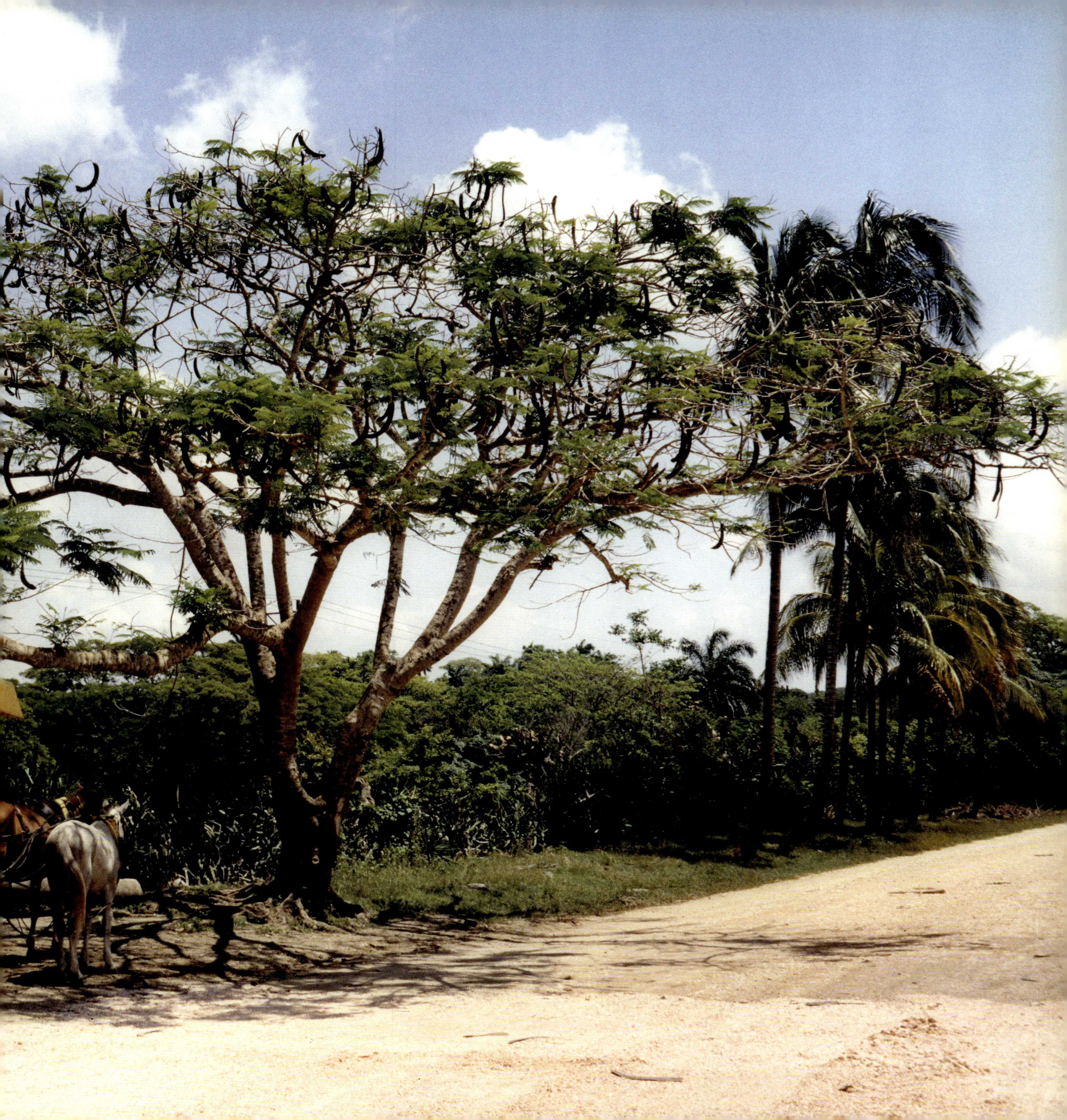

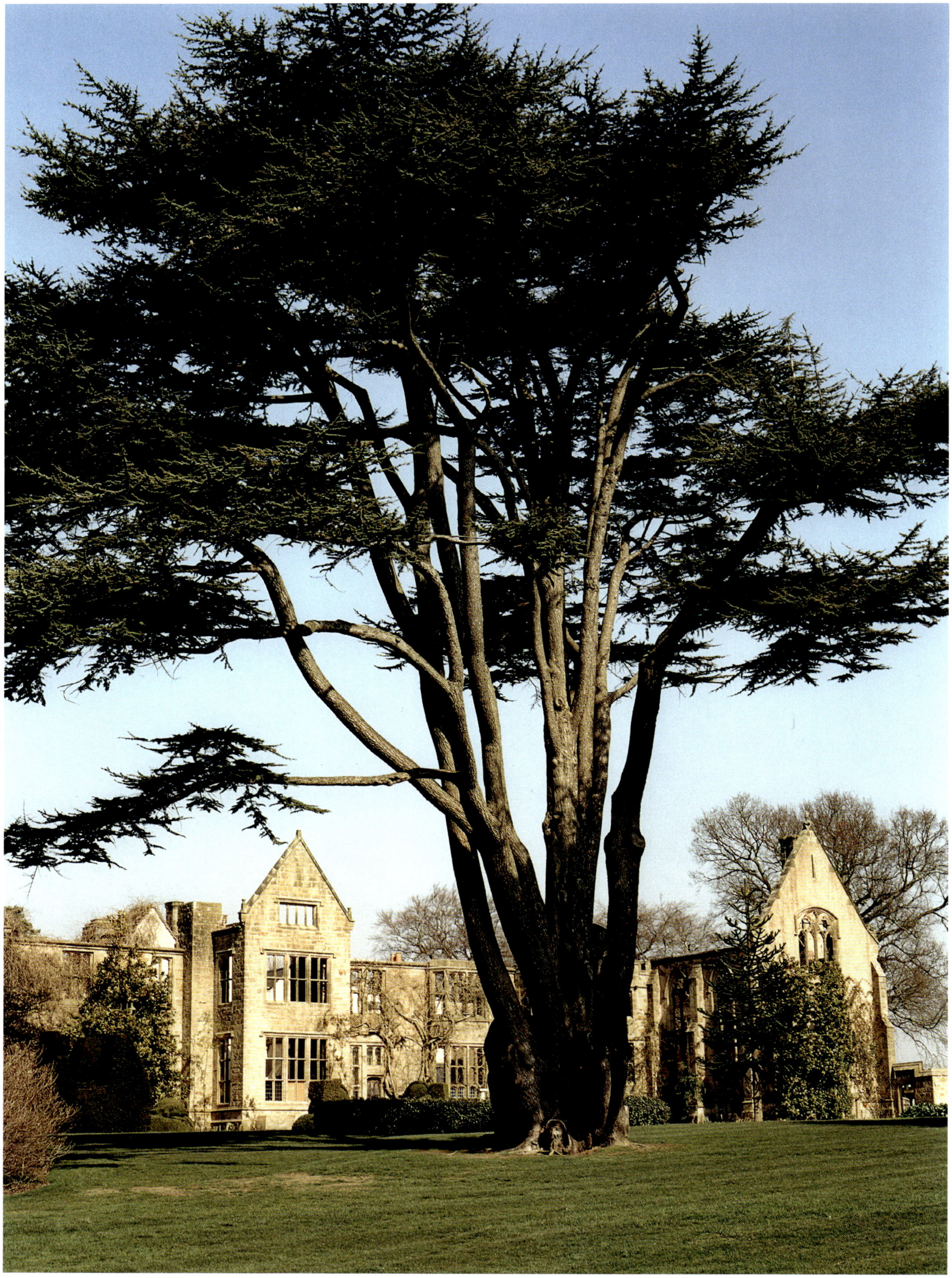

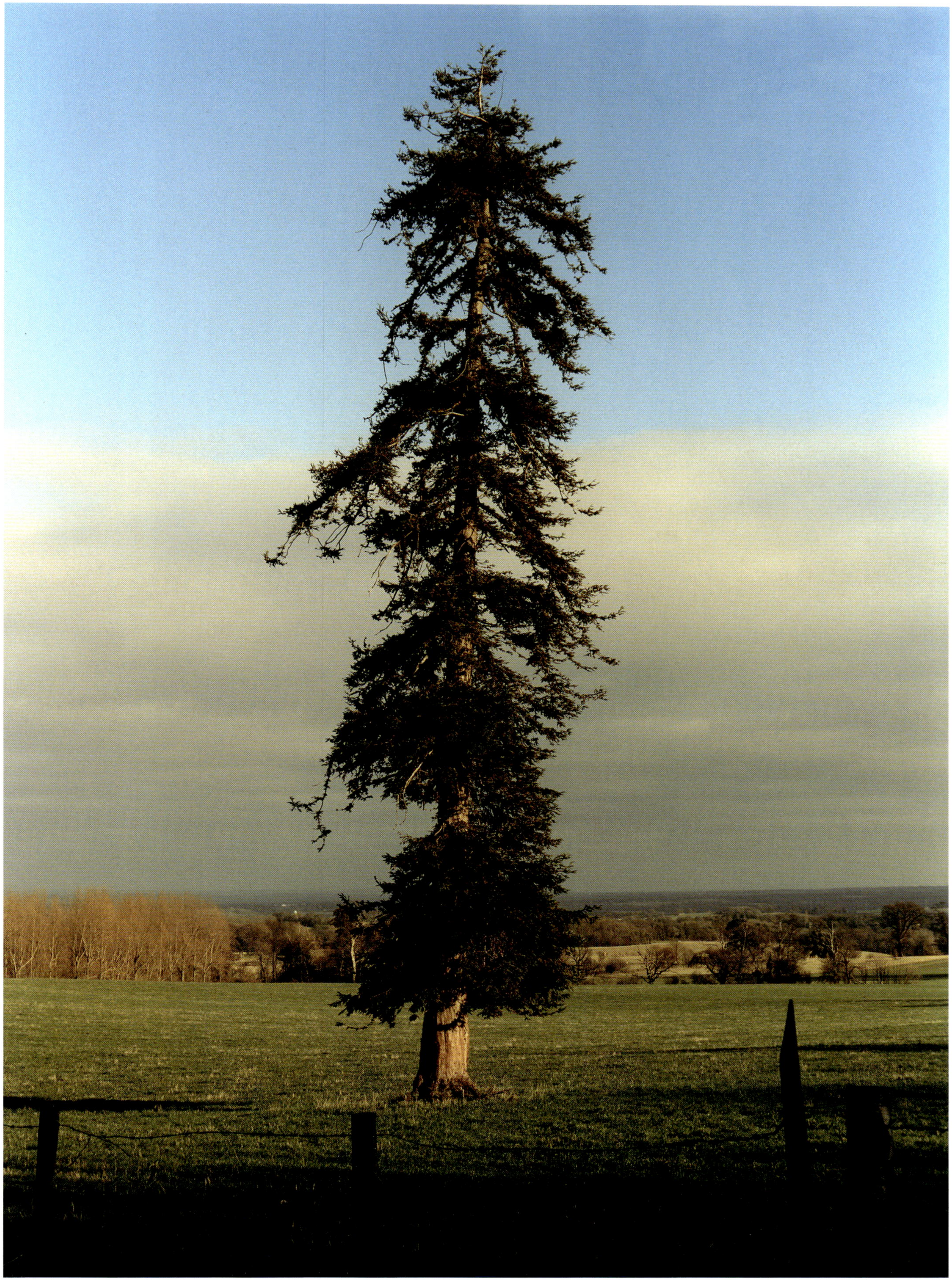

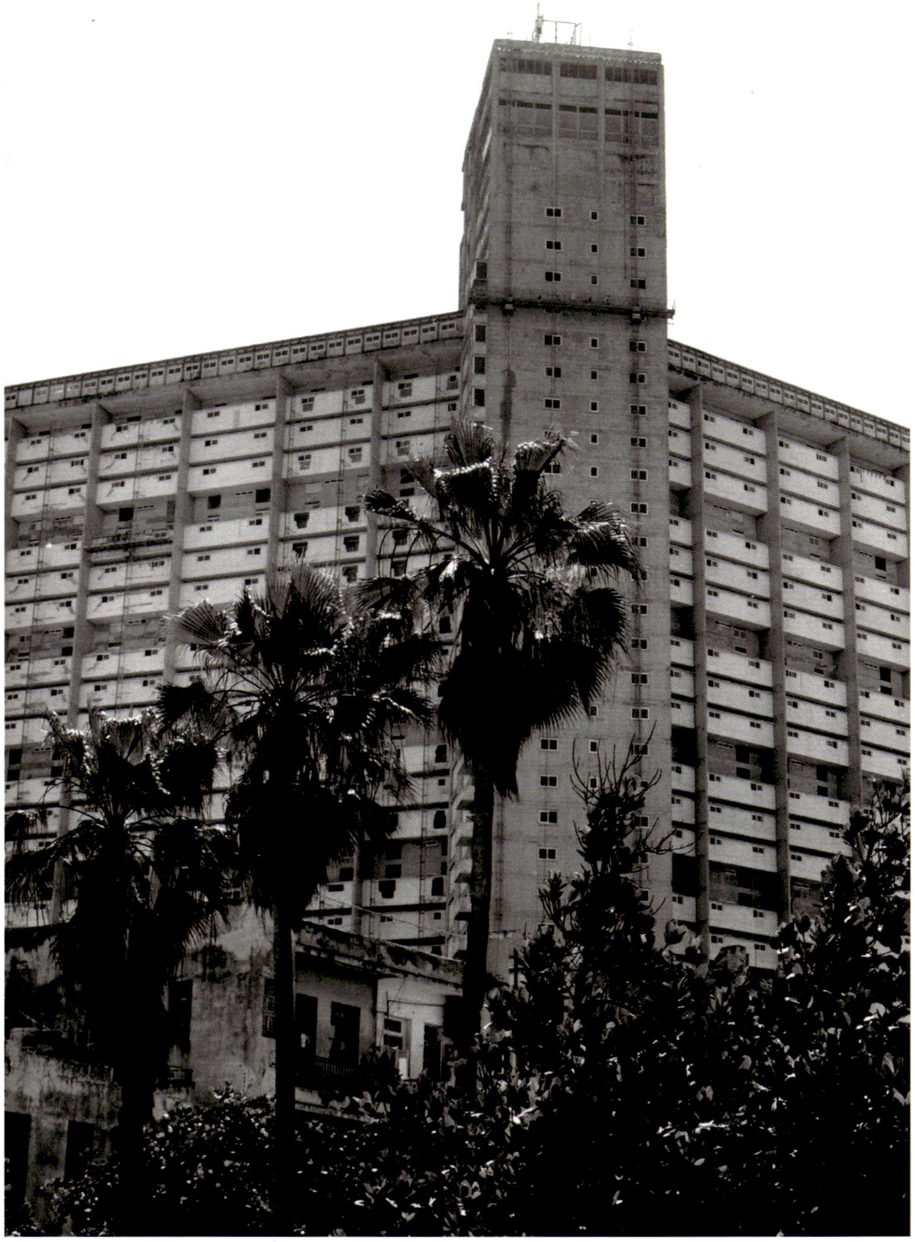

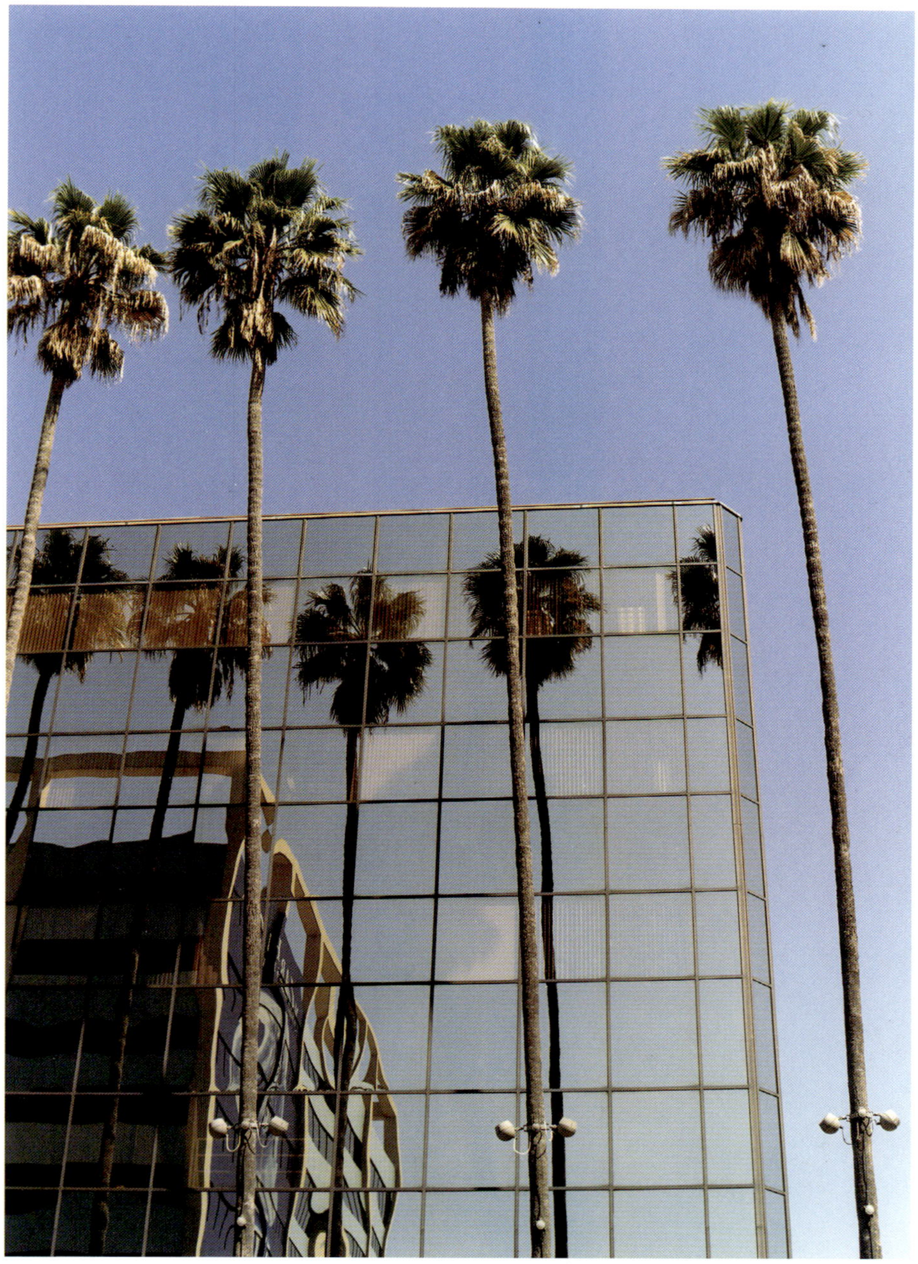

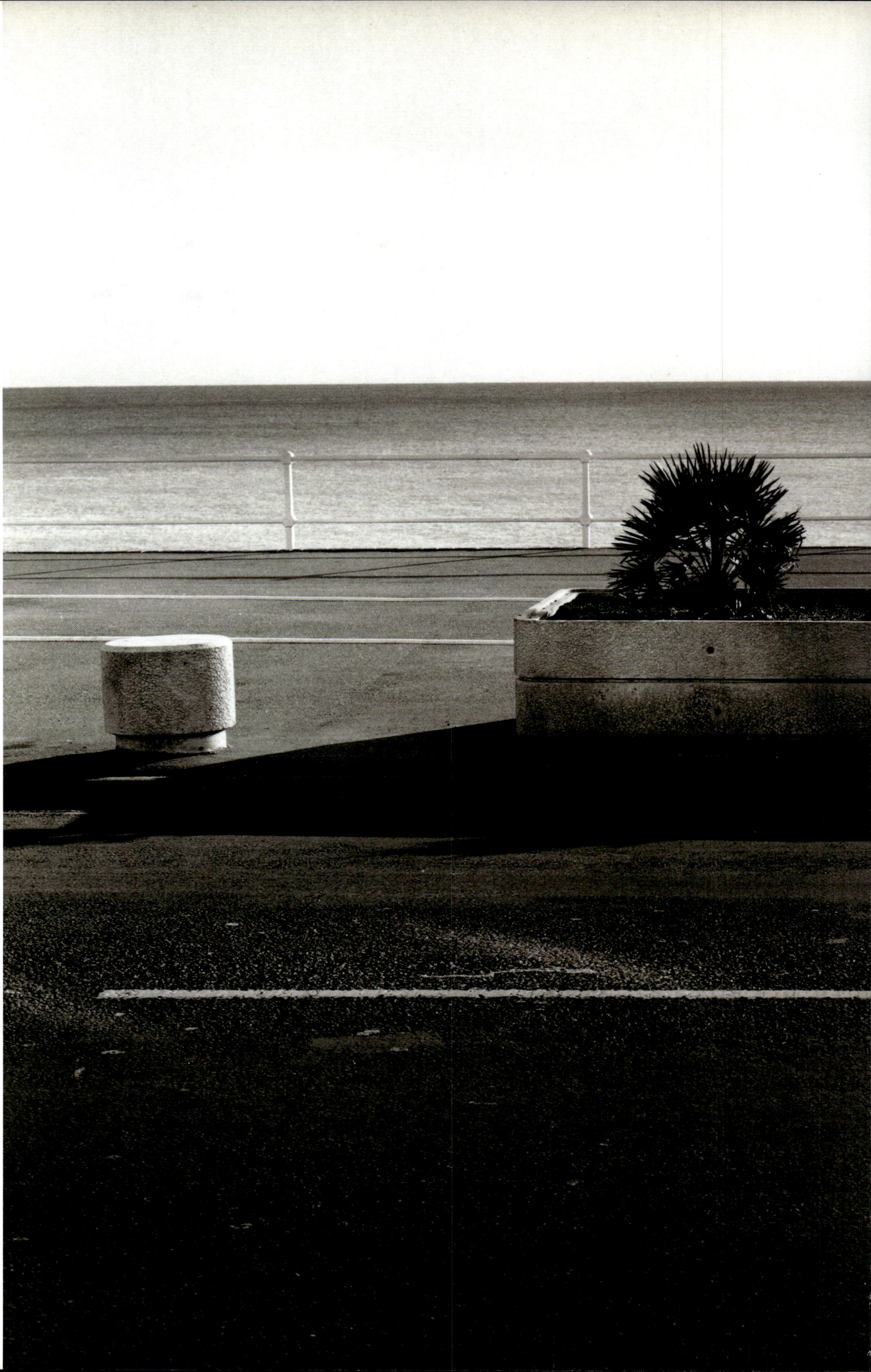

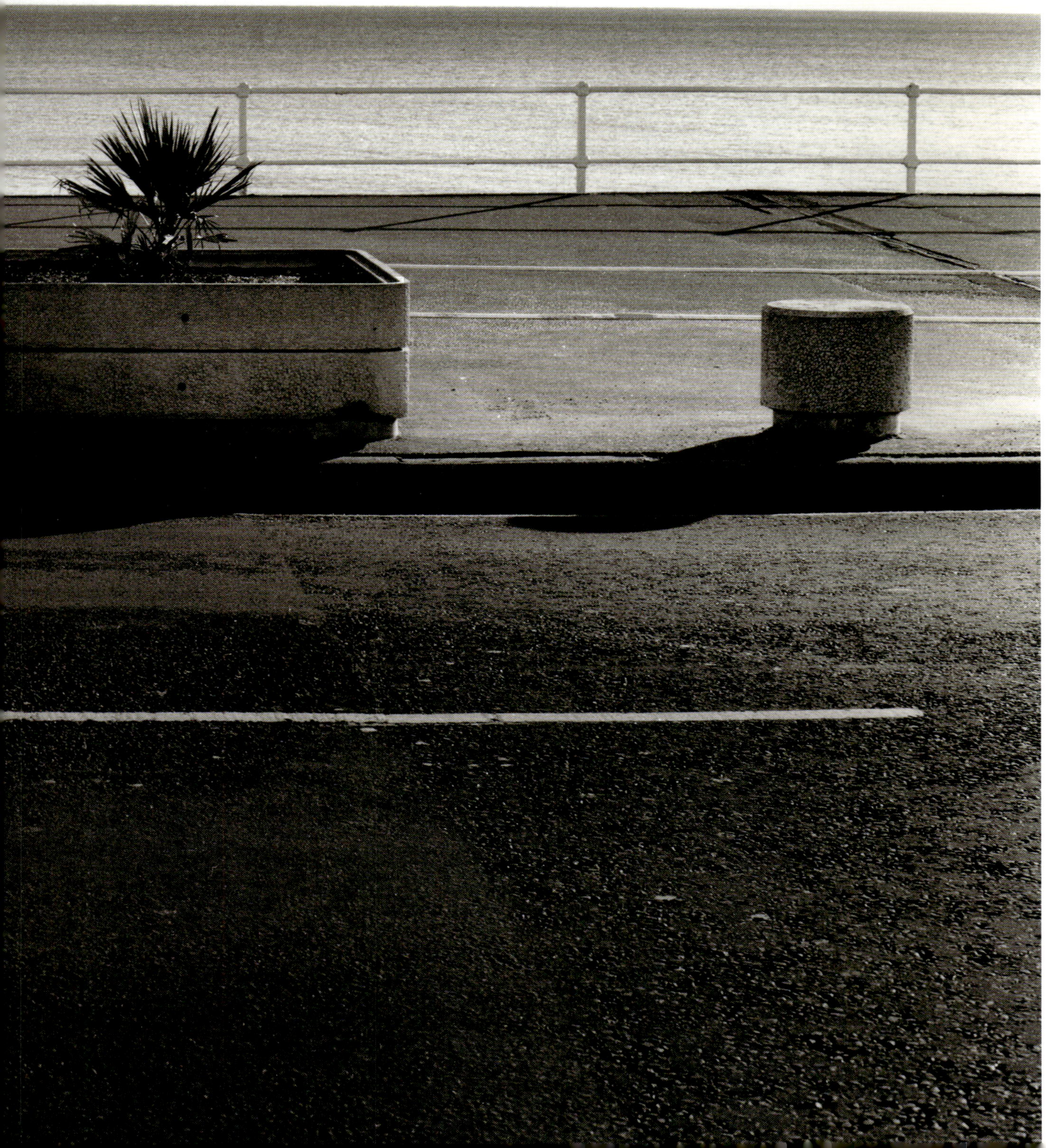

Suburbia is where the developer bulldozes out the trees,
then names the streets after them.

Bill Vaughan 1915-1977

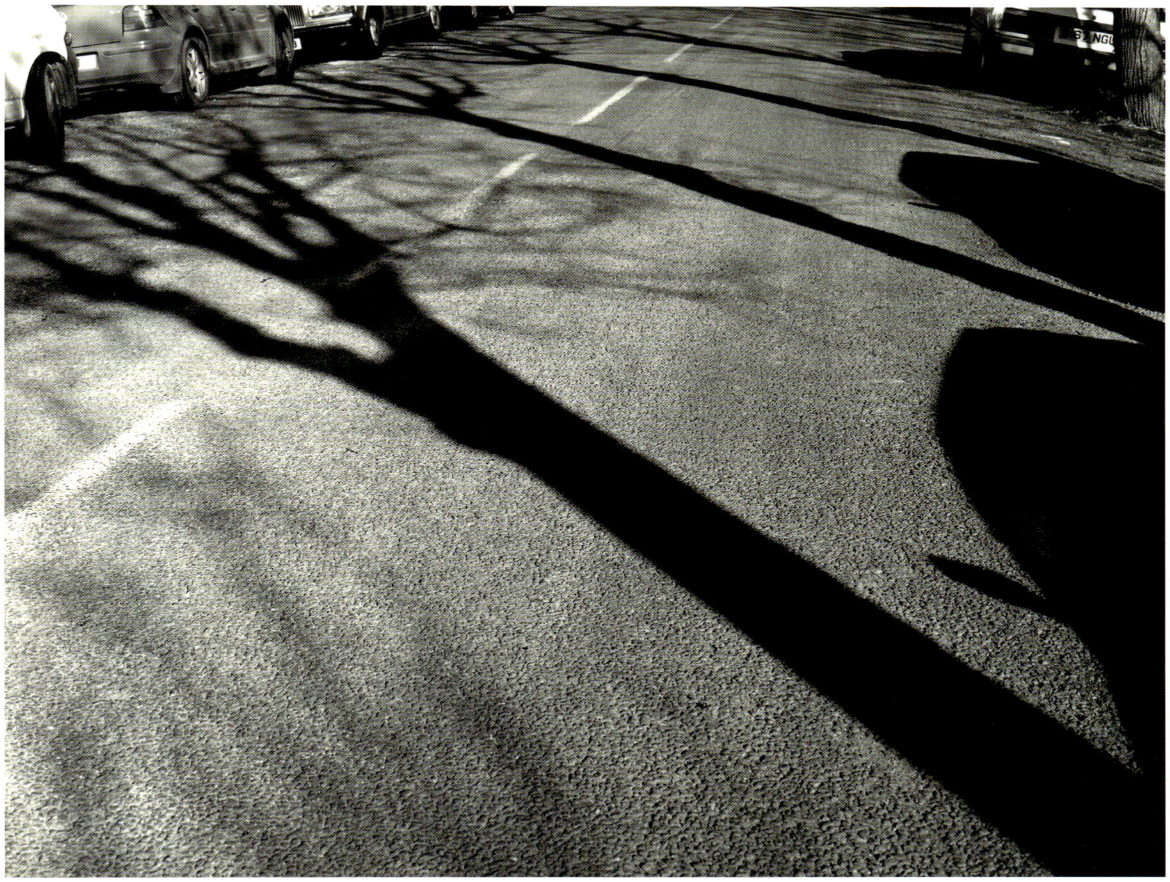

He that plants trees loves others beside himself.

Thomas Fuller, 1608-1661

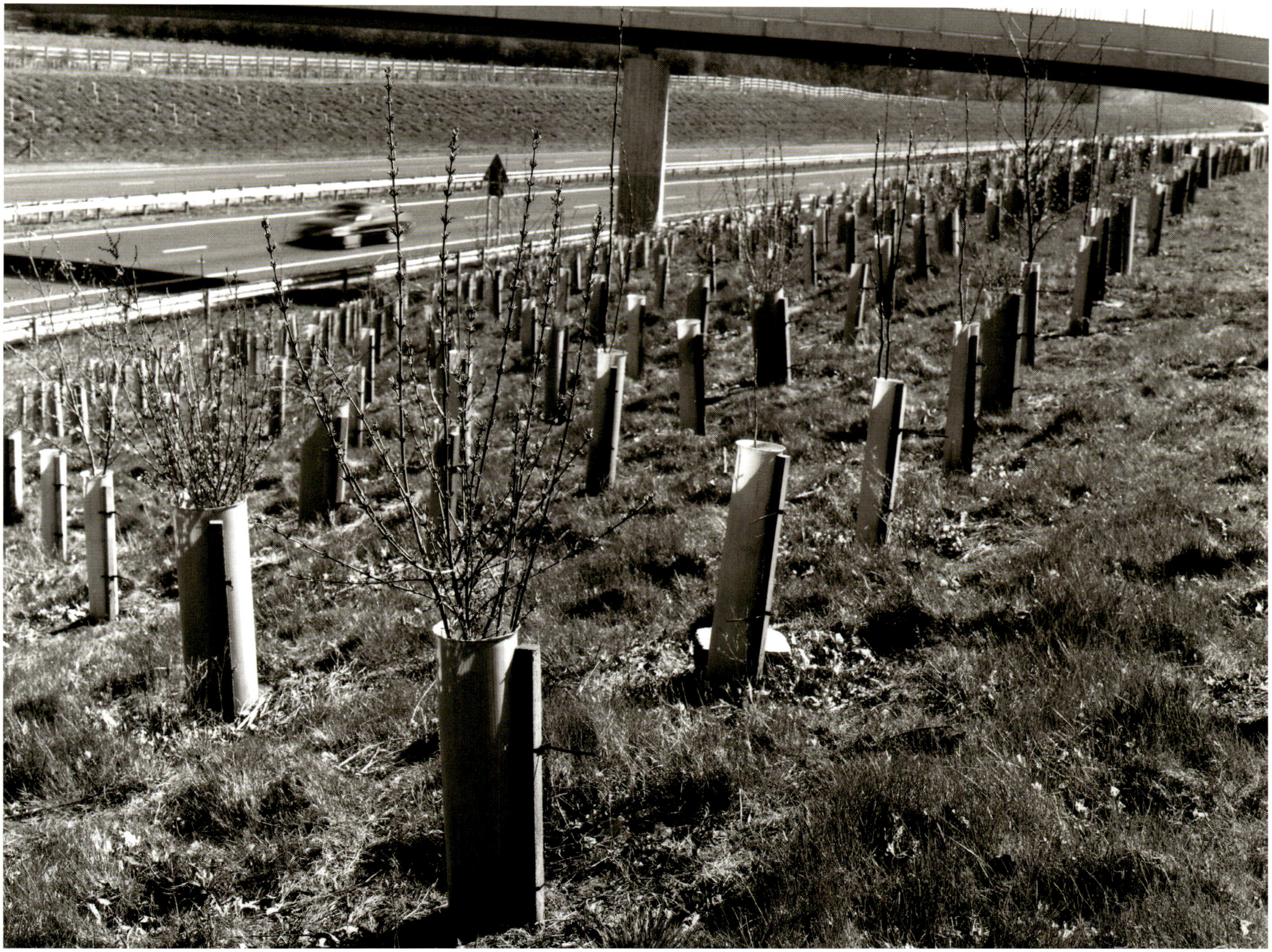

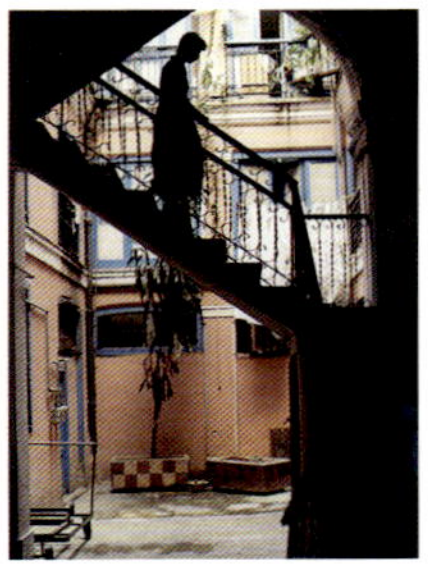
Courtyard Palm
Havana, Cuba.

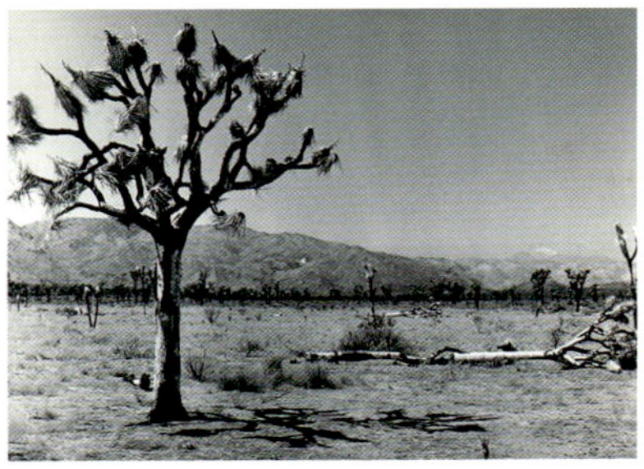
Burned Joshua Trees,
California, USA.

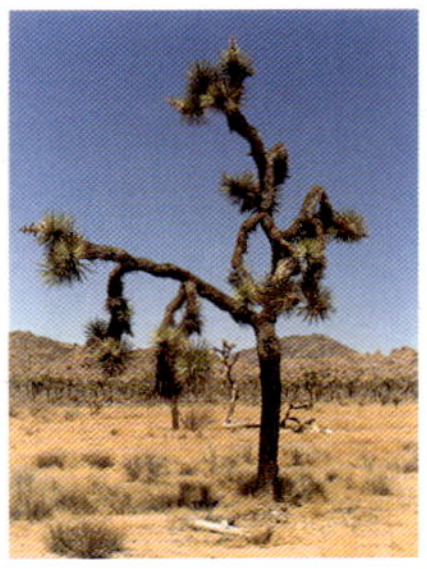
Joshua Tree,
California, USA

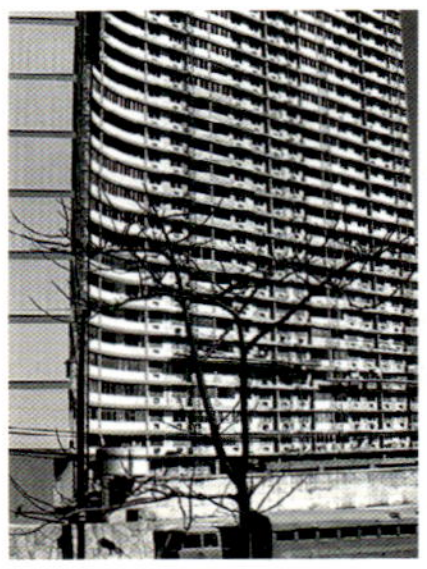
Focsa Building and Tree,
Havana, Cuba.

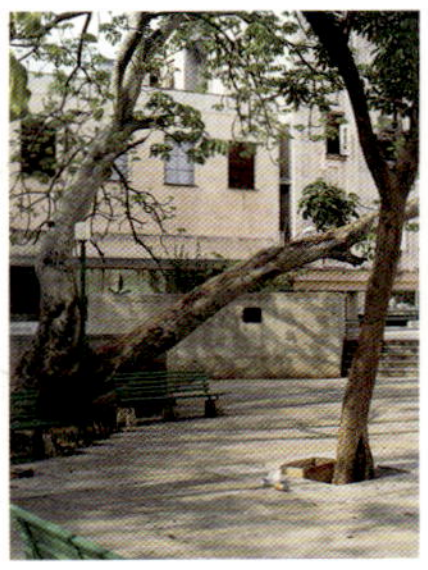
Encased Trees,
Havana, Cuba.

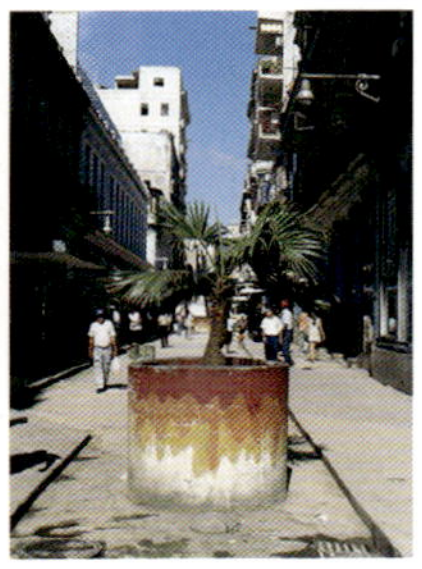
Planted Palm,
Havana, Cuba.

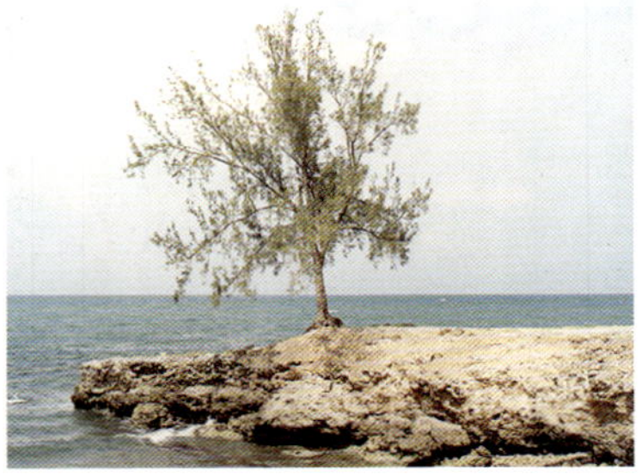
Tree on Rock,
Gibara, Cuba.

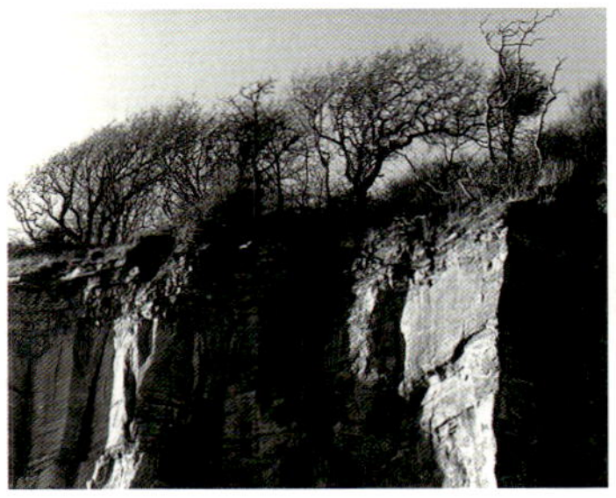
Trees on Chalky Cliffs,
Kent, UK.

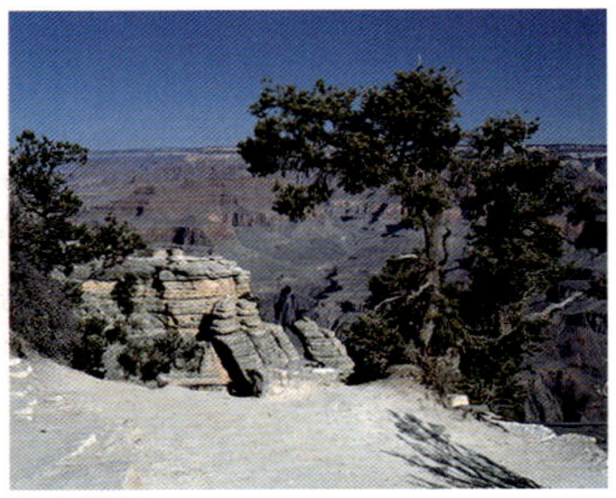
Spruce at the Edge of the Grand Canyon,
Arizona, USA.

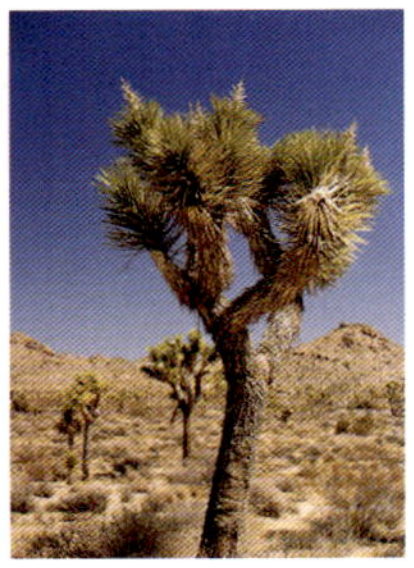
Green Joshua Tree,
California, USA

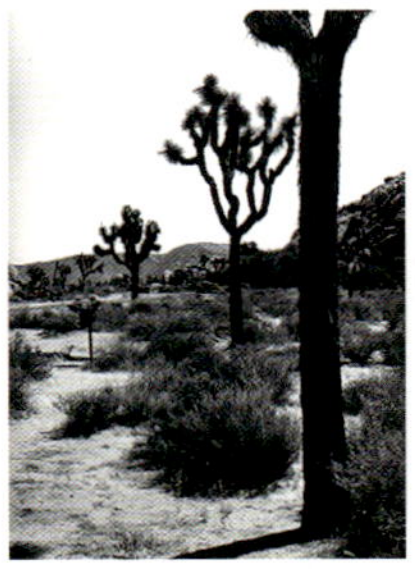
Joshua Tree Park,
California, USA

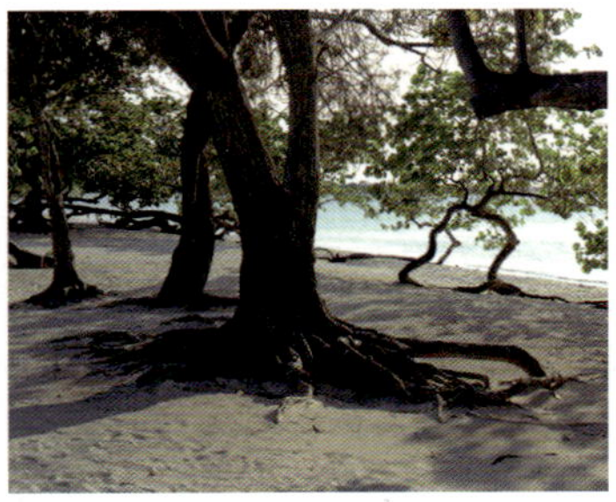
Mangroves in Sand,
Guardalavaca, Cuba.

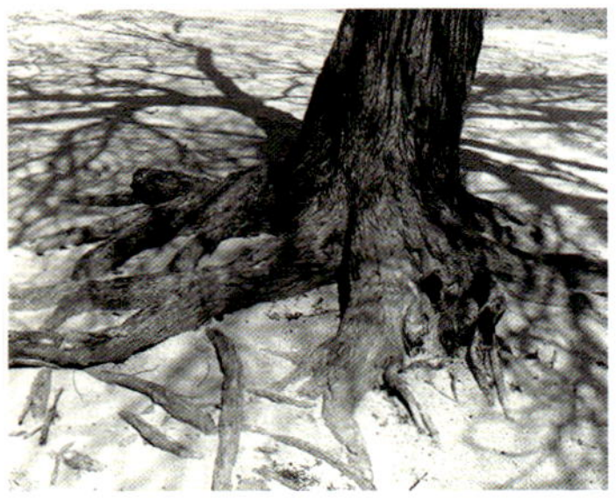
Tree Roots in Sand,
Guardalavaca,Cuba.

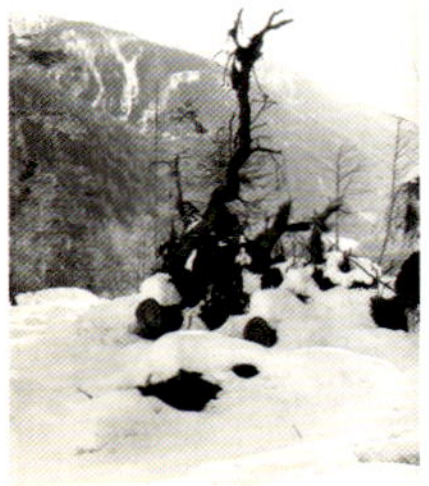
Pine Tree Roots,
South Tirol, Italy.

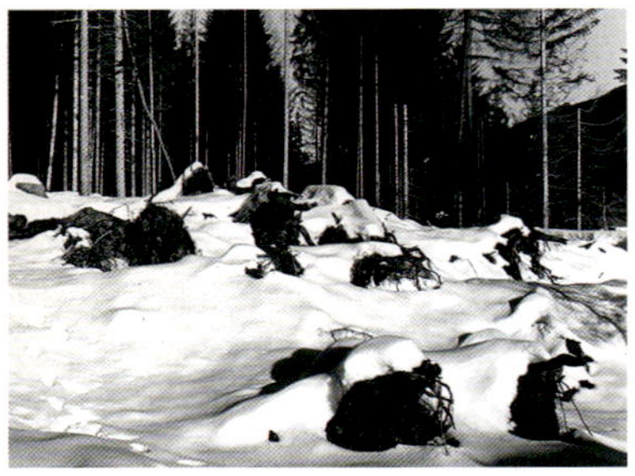
Avalanche Uprooted Pine Trees,
South Tirol, Italy.

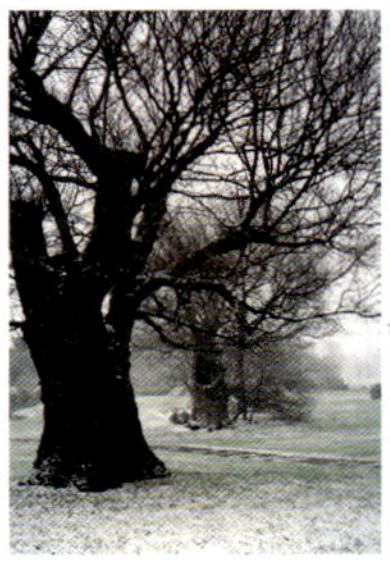
Oldest Surviving Elms,
East Sussex, UK

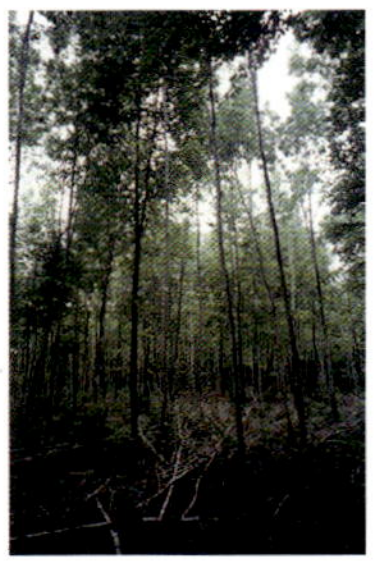
Thin Beech Wood,
West Sussex, UK

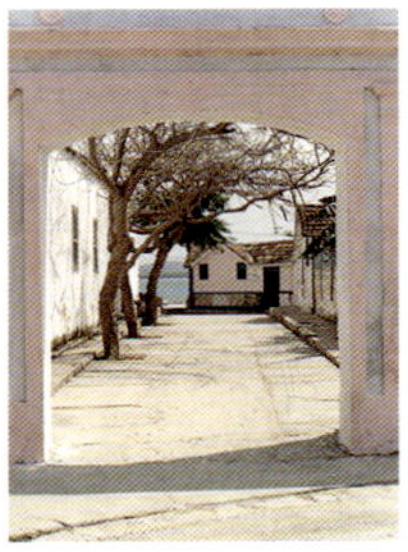
Pink Arch with Trees,
Gibara, Cuba

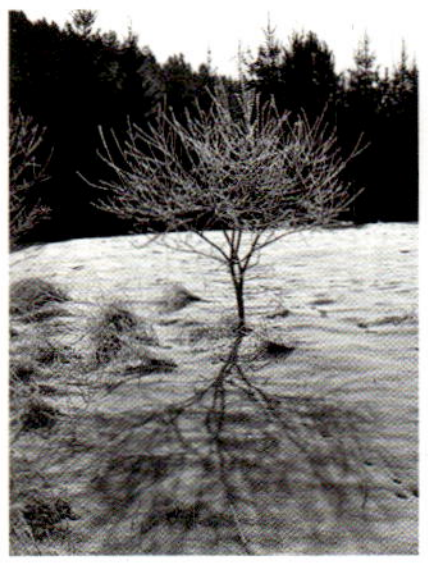
Icy Tree,
Bavaria, Germany.

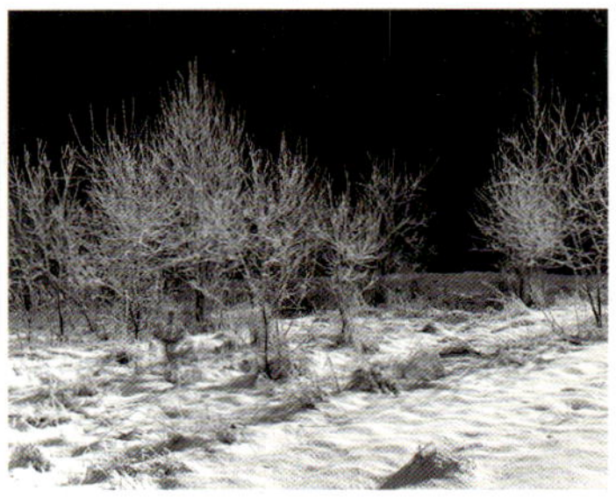
Group of Icy Trees,
Bavaria, Germany.

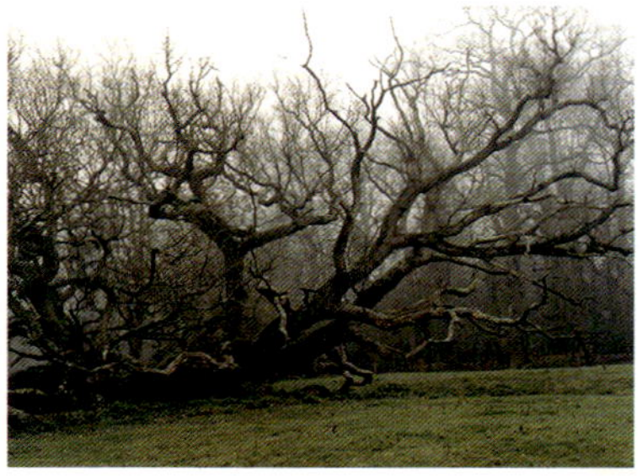
Fallen Oak,
Sussex, UK.

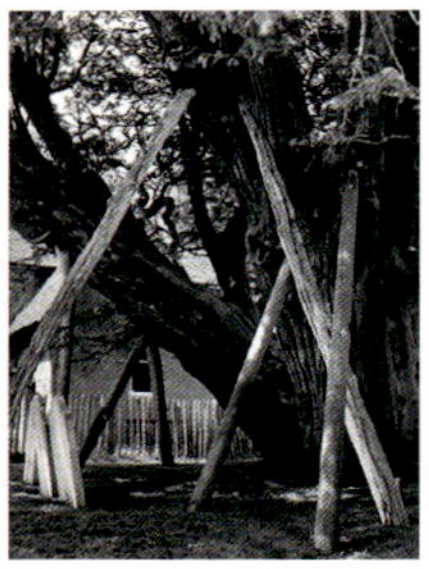
1400 Year Old Willow Tree,
Kent, UK.

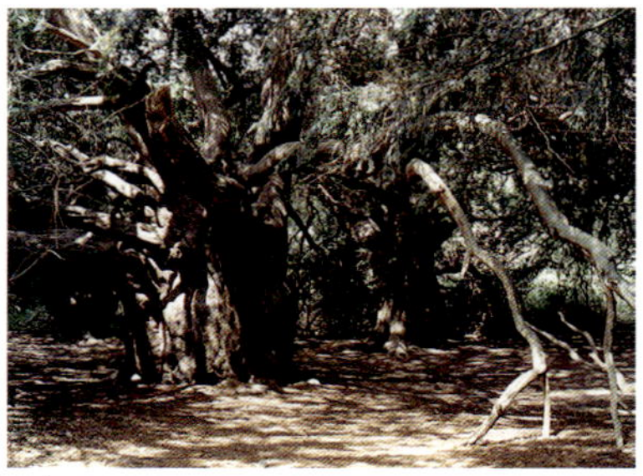
Oldest Yew Forest in Europe, *4000 Years*,
West Sussex, UK.

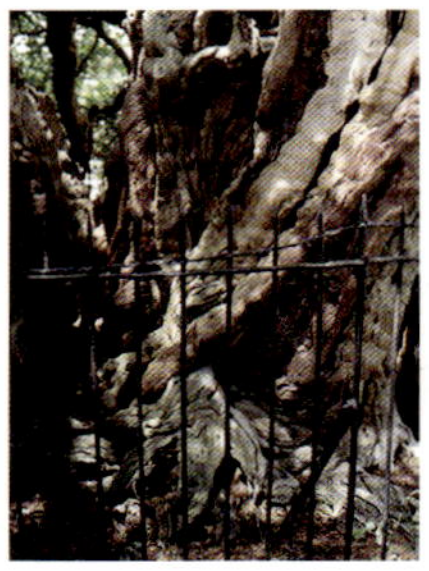
1200 Year Old Yew Tree,
Kent, UK.

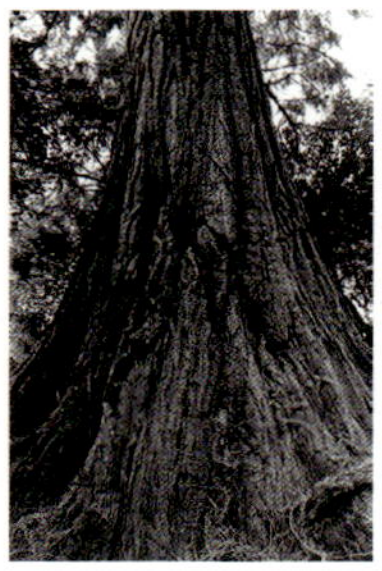
Redwood Tree,
Sussex, UK.

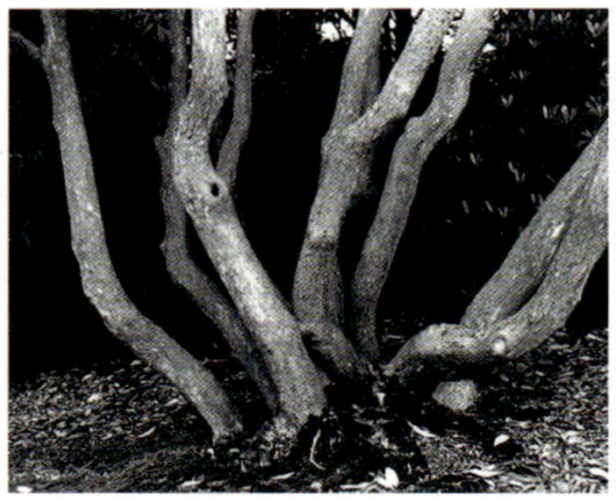
7 Legged Tree,
Sussex, UK.

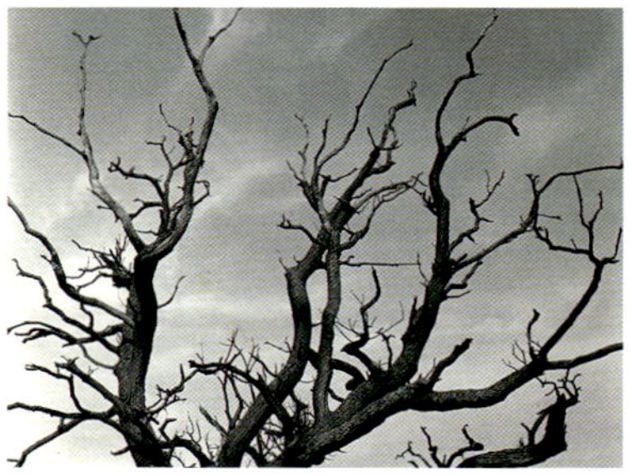
Dead Oak,
Kent, UK.

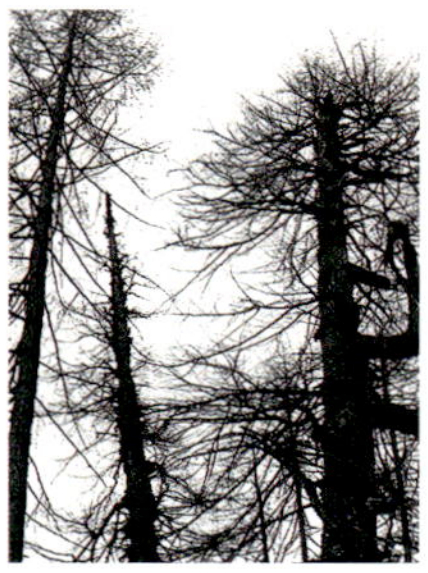
Oldest Larch Trees in
Europe, South Tirol, Italy.

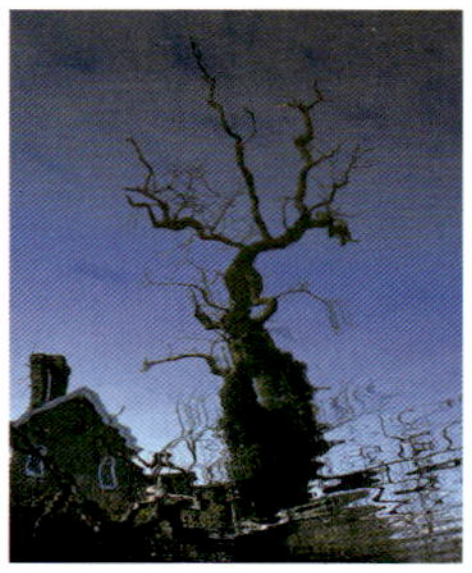
Old Oak
East Sussex, UK.

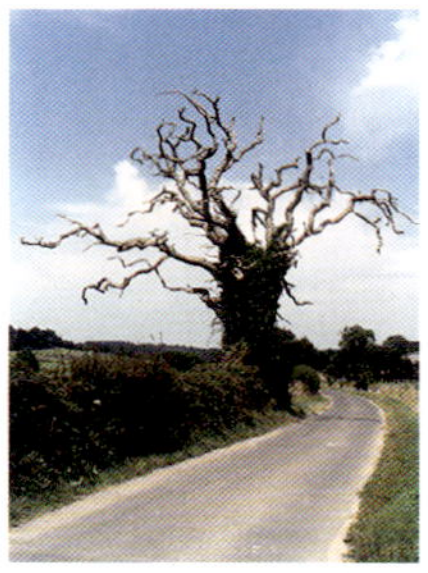
Dead Oak with Ivy,
West Sussex, UK.

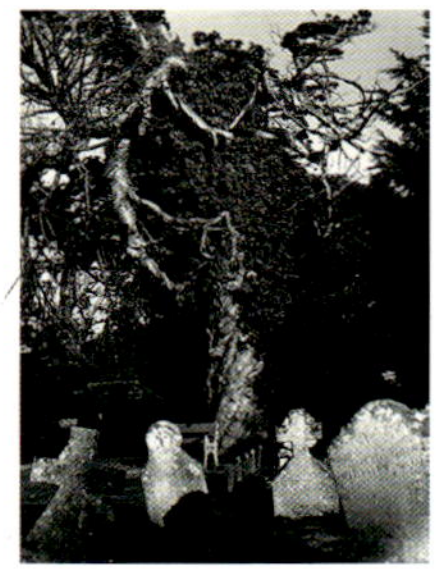
Yew Tree with Ivy,
West Sussex, UK.

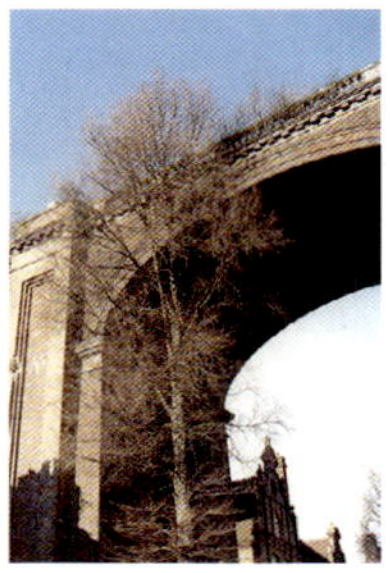
Scarlet Oak,
East Sussex, UK.

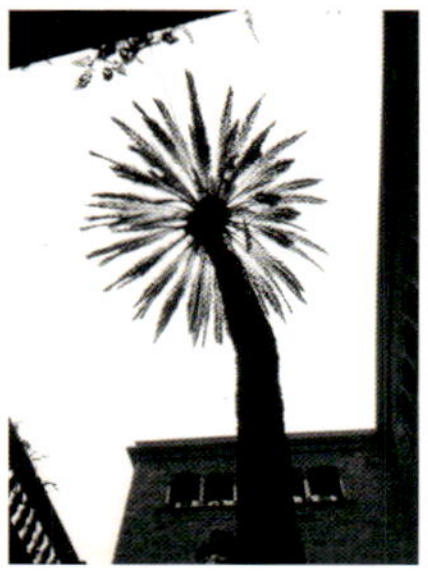
Palm in Courtyard,
Barcelona, Spain.

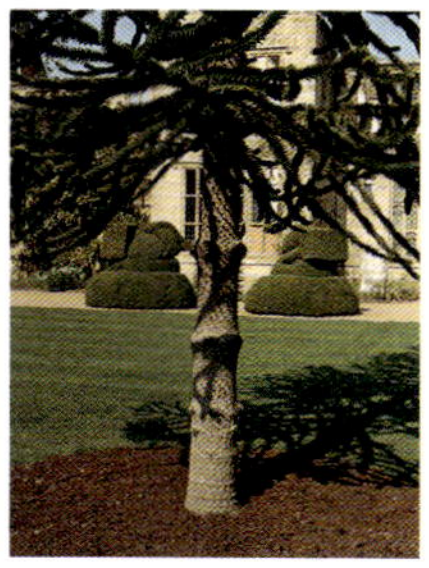
Monkey Puzzle and
Clipped Yews, Sussex, UK.

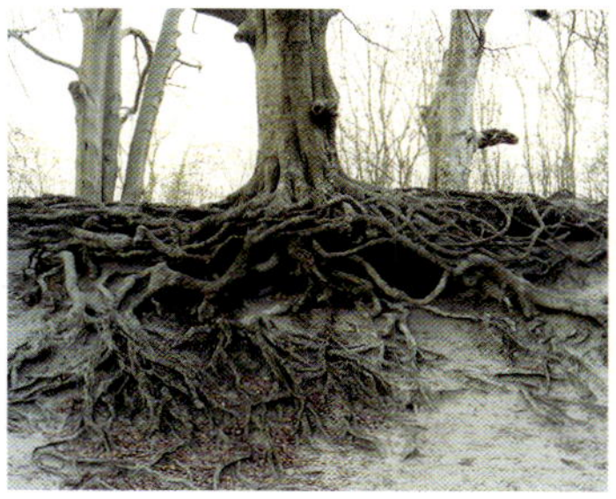
Beech Tree Roots,
East Sussex, UK.

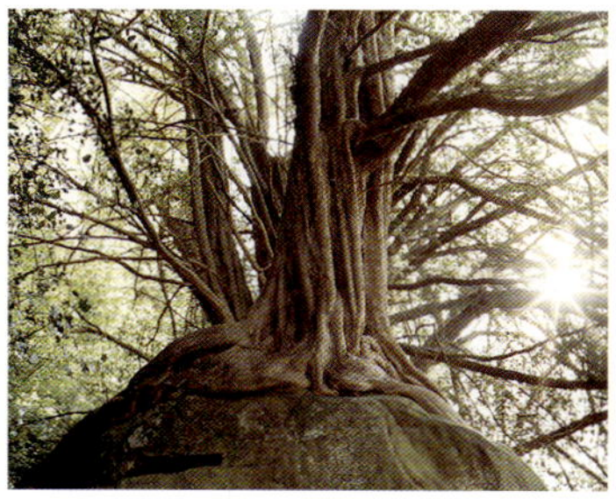
Yew on Rock,
Kent, UK.

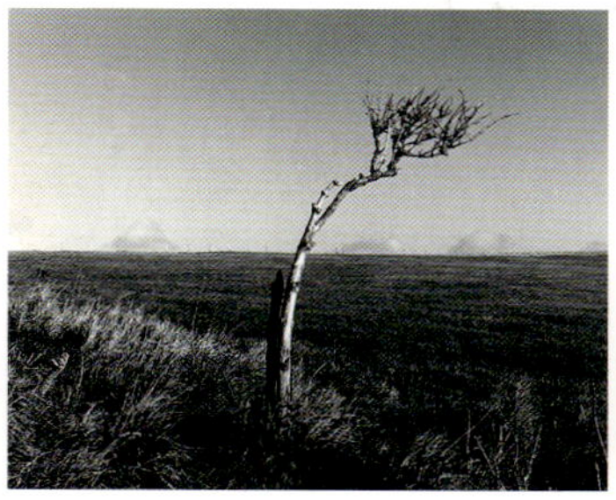
Single Coastal Tree,
East Sussex, UK.

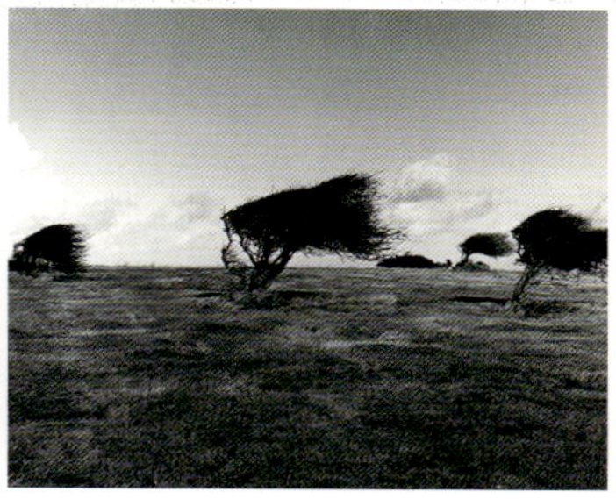
Wind Blown Coastal Trees,
East Sussex, UK.

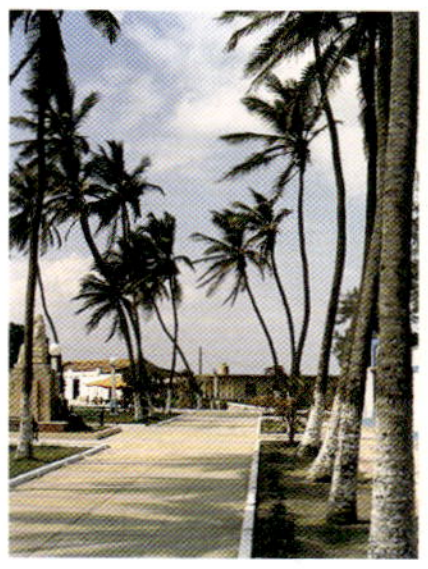
Wind Blown Palms,
Gibara, Cuba.

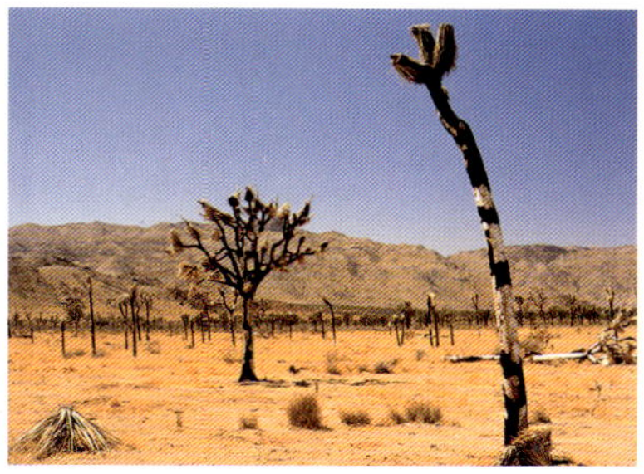
Burned Joshua Trees,
California, USA.

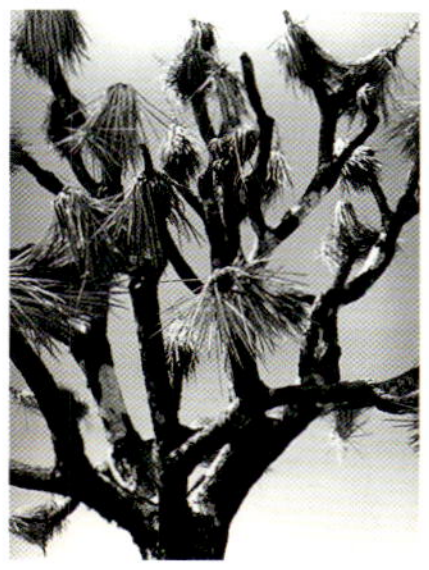
Burned Joshua Tree,
California,USA.

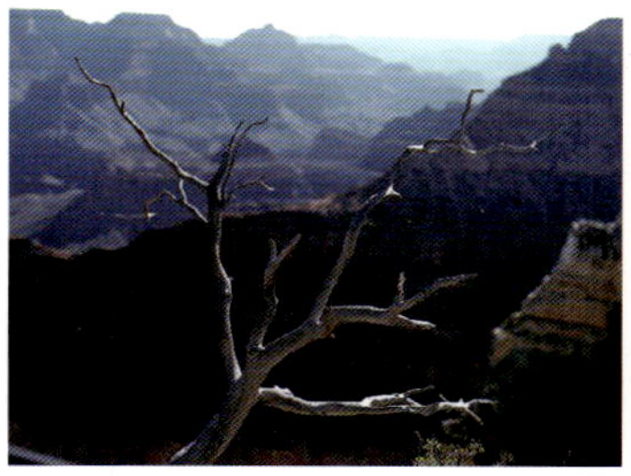
Dead Tree in Grand Canyon,
Arizona, USA.

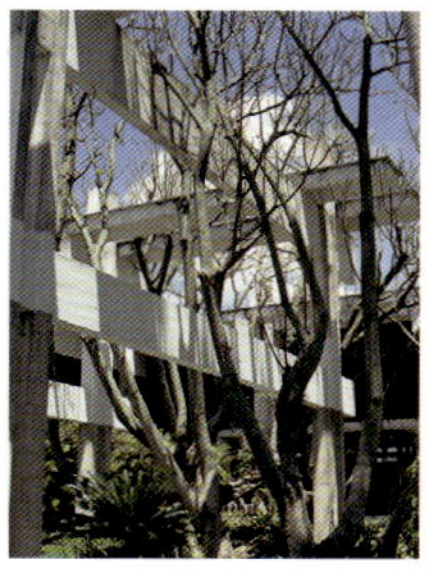
Las Ruinas, Old Sugarmill
and Trees, Havana, Cuba.

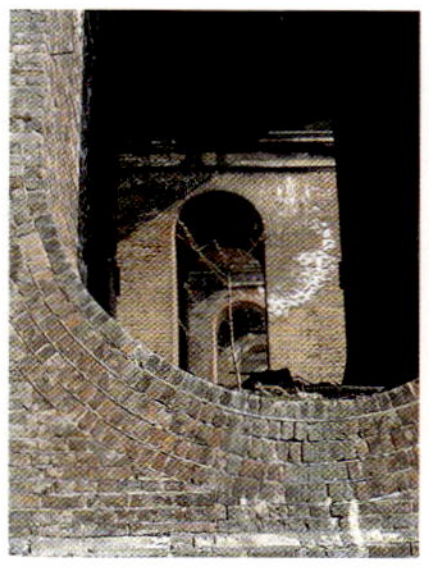
Tree in Spring under the
Arches, East Sussex, UK.

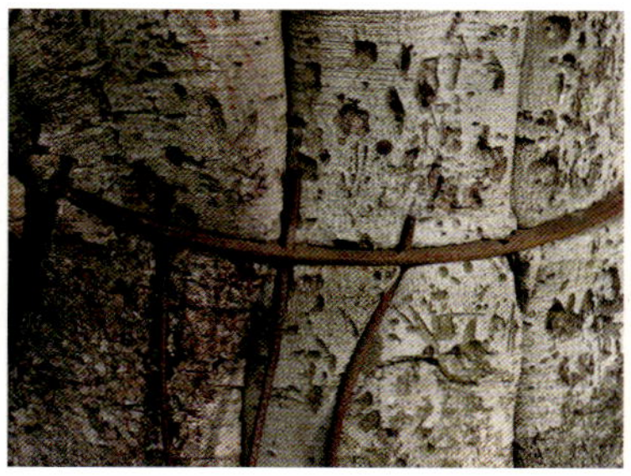
Beech Tree with Ingrown Fence,
Sussex, UK.

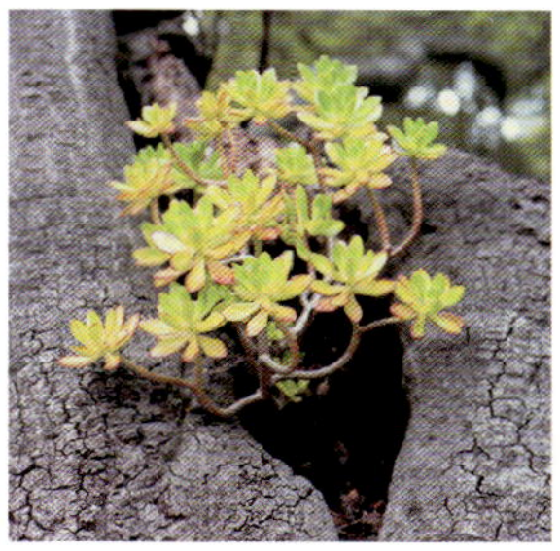
Succulent growing in Tree,
California, USA.

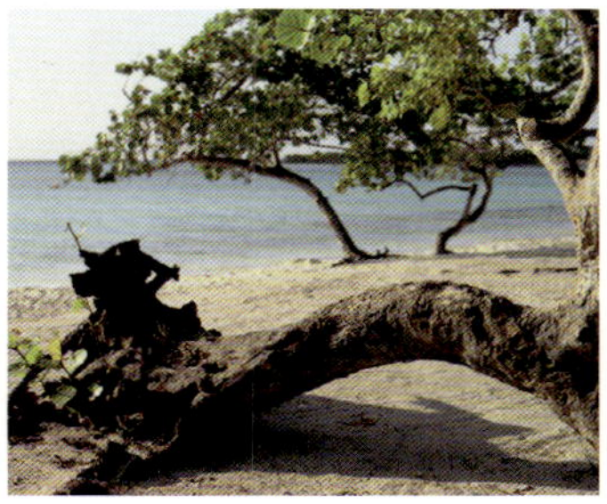
Fallen Mangrove,
Guardalavaca,Cuba.

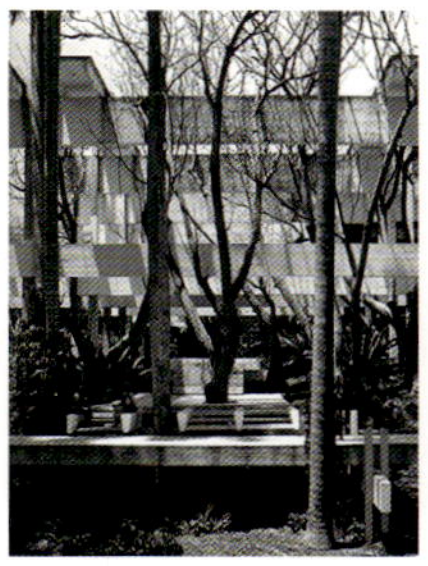
Las Ruinas, Built in 1971 by
Joaquin Galvan, Cuba.

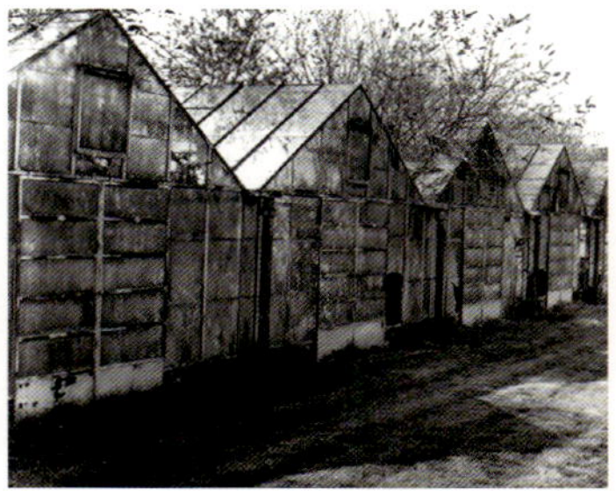
Derelict Plantations,
Sussex, UK.

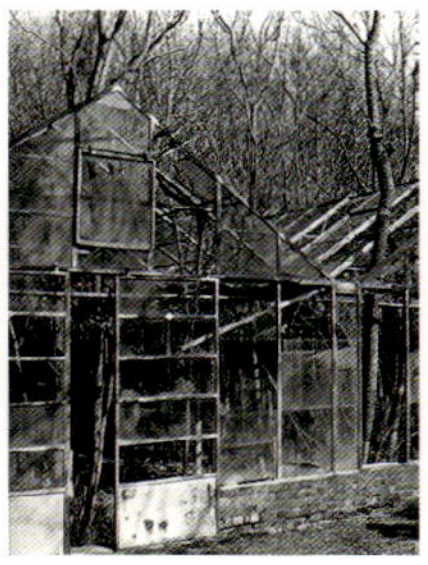
Trees in Derelict Greenhouse,
Sussex, UK.

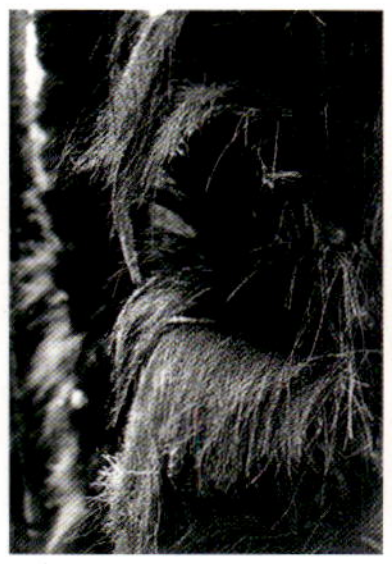
Fury Palm Close Up,
Kent, UK.

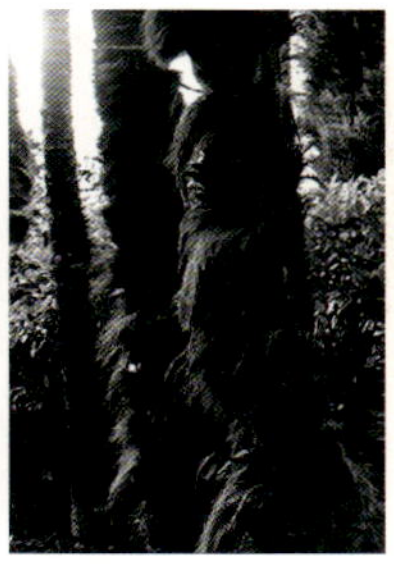
Palm Trunks,
Kent, UK.

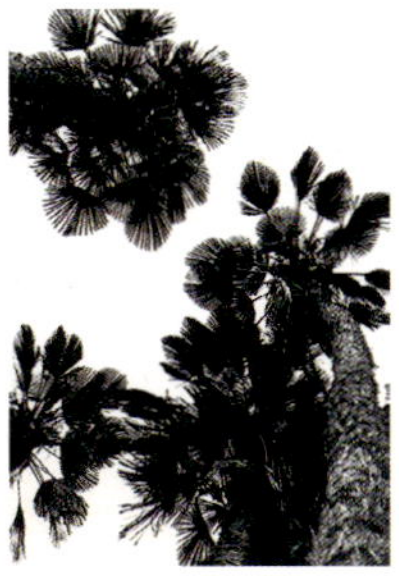
Palm Tree Tops,
Kent, UK.

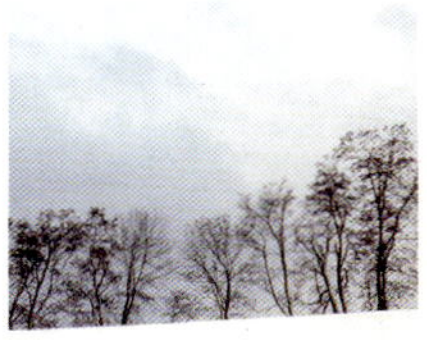
Snowy Tree Line,
Bavaria, Germany.

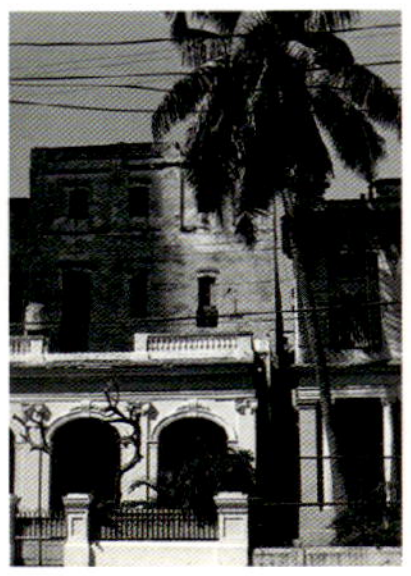
Palm in Front Garden,
Havana, Cuba.

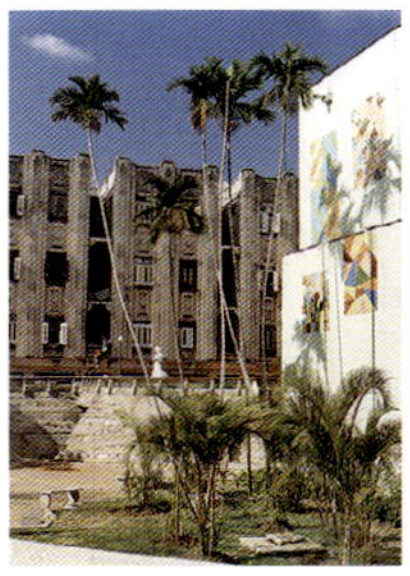
Thin Palms,
Havana, Cuba.

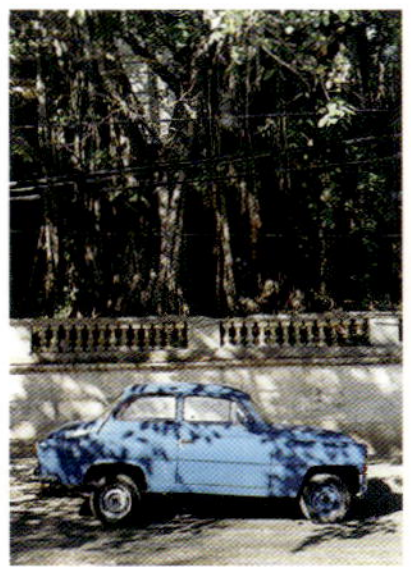
Banyan Tree,
Havana, Cuba.

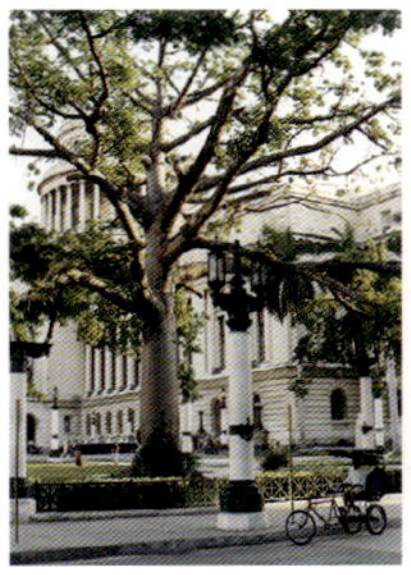
Big Birch,
Central Havana, Cuba.

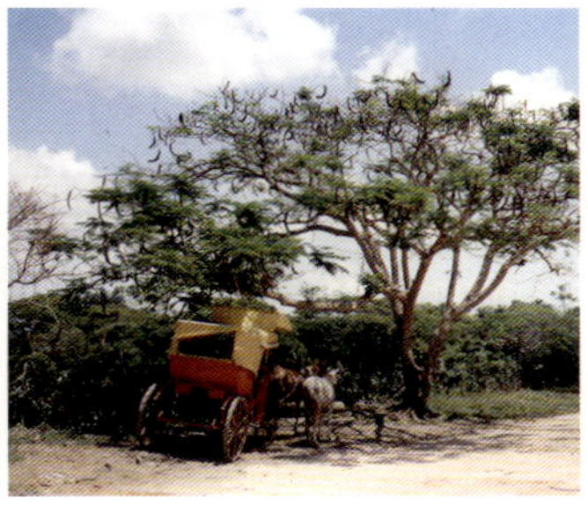
Coach and Carob Tree,
Holguin, Cuba.

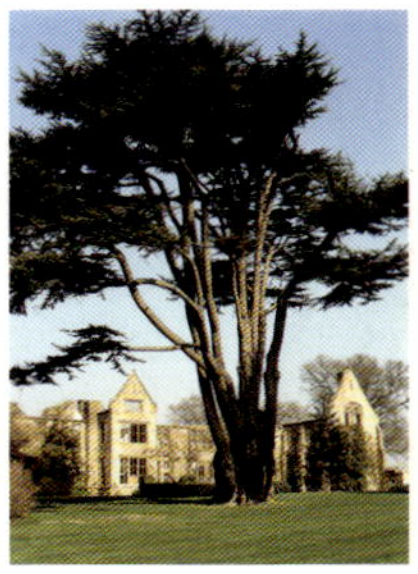
Cedar of Lebanon,
Sussex, UK.

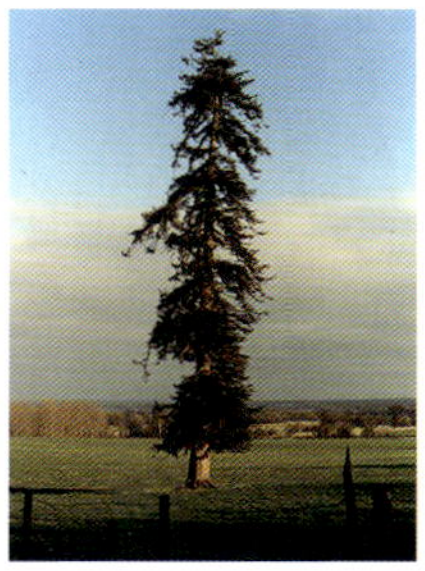
Big Fir,
Sussex, UK.

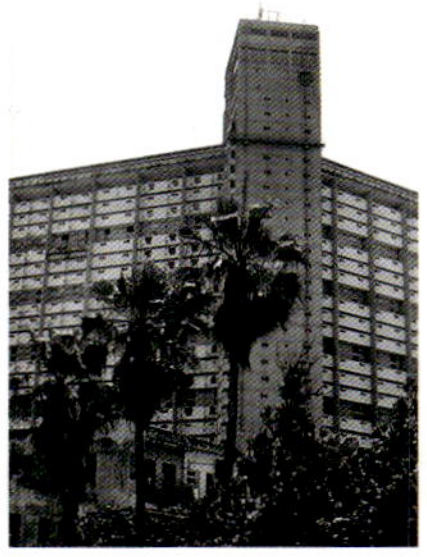
3 Palms Focsa Building,
Havana, Cuba.

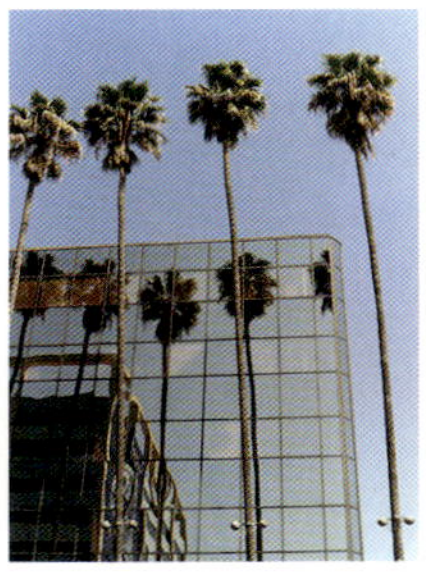
Los Angeles Palms,
California, USA.

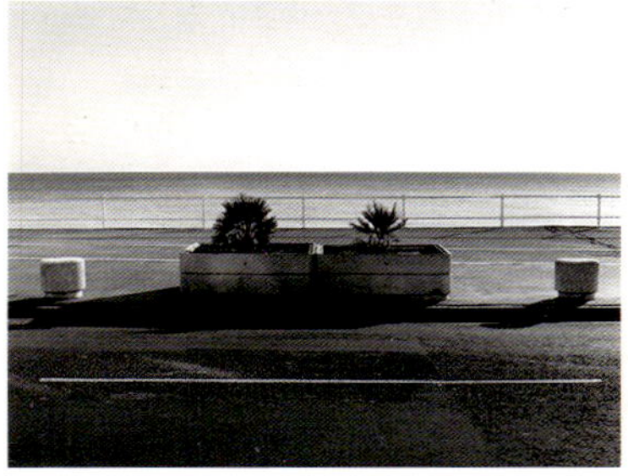
Planted Palms,
Kent, UK.

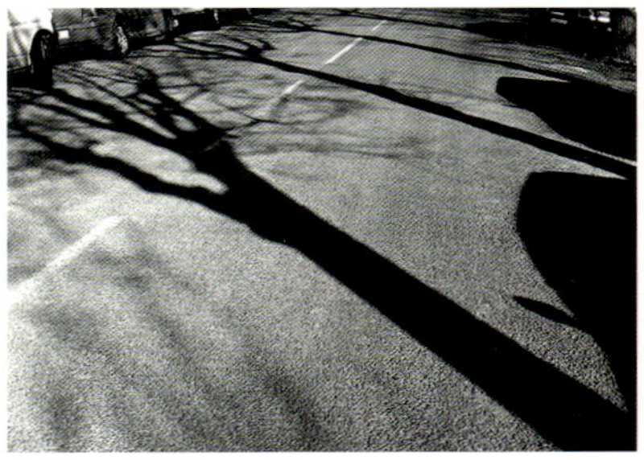
Suburban Shadow Trees,
East Sussex, UK.

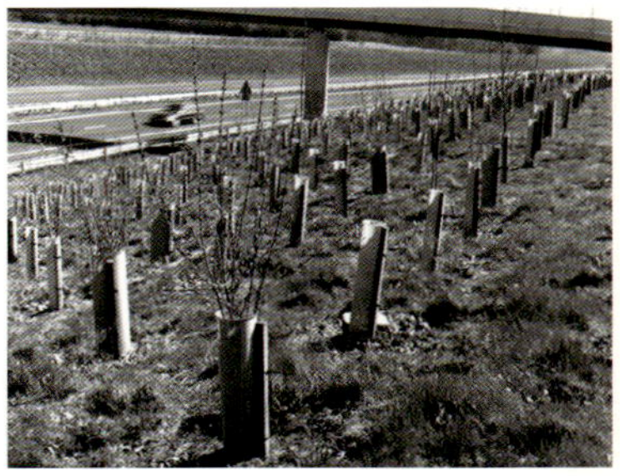
New Tree Planting,
Kent, UK.

Dedicated to
Werner and Winnie Haverich

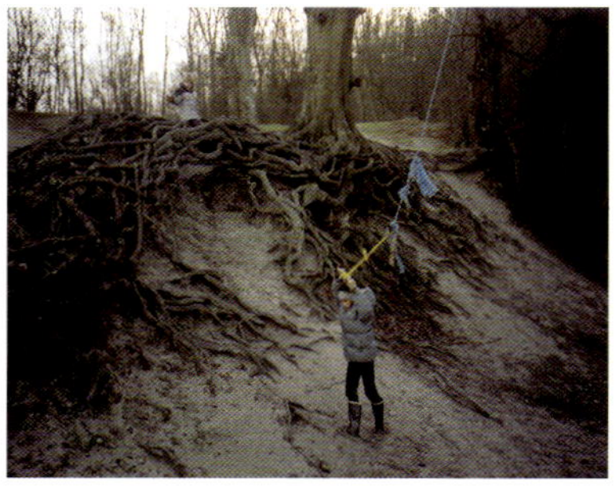

Thank you to my family for their patience and discovering some of these amazing trees with me!

A special thank you to Jon Snow for his foreword and his continuing support of my book.

A big thank you to Betty and David Kerr and to my husband David for their kind help and contributions.

A sincere thank you to:

Robert Horne Group and their Mill for the donation of the Revive Silk Paper.
Mary Warren
Tim Smith

Brighton University
George Hardie
Karen Norquay
Jackie Batey

Damiani Editore
Giuseppe Villirillo

Also thank you to Veena and Natalia my best friends for their encouragement, and to all the other friends that helped me out.

www.beatricehaverich.com

Printed in Italy, June 2006
Grafiche Damiani s.r.l.
www.grafichedamiani.it